بسم الله الرحمن الرحيم

IN THE NAME OF ALLAH,
THE ALL-BENEFICENT, THE ALL-MERCIFUL

قال الله تعالى:

﴿إِنَّمَا يُرِيدُ اللَّهُ لِيُذْهِبَ عَنْكُمُ الرِّجْسَ أَهْلَ الْبَيْتِ وَيُطَهِّرَكُمْ تَطْهِيرًا﴾

Indeed, Allah desires to repel all impurity from you, O People of the Household, and purify you with a thorough purification.
(*Sūrat al-Aḥzāb* 33:33).

Prophetic traditions, mentioned in most reliable Sunnī and Shī'īte reference books of *ḥadīth* and *tafsīr* (Qur'anic Exegesis), confirm that this holy verse was revealed to exclusively involve the five People of the Cloak; namely, Muḥammad, 'Alī, Fāṭimah, al-Ḥasan, and al-Ḥusayn, peace be upon them, to whom the term 'Ahl al-Bayt (People of the House)' is solely dedicated.

For instance, refer to the following references:

(1) Aḥmad ibn Ḥanbal (d. 241 AH), *al-Musnad*, 1:331; 4:107; 6:292, 304. (2) *Ṣaḥīḥ Muslim* (d. 261 AH), 7:130. (3) At-Tirmidhī (d. 279 AH), *Sunan*, 5:361 et al. (4) Ad-Dūlābī (d. 310 AH), *adh-Dhurriyyah aṭ-Ṭāhirah an-Nabawiyyah*, p. 108. (5) An-Nassā'ī (d. 303 AH), *as-Sunan al-Kubrā'*, 5: p. 108, 113. (6) Al-Ḥākim an-Naysābūrī (d. 405 AH), *al-Mustadrak 'ala'ṣ-Ṣaḥīḥayn*, 2:416, 3:133, 146, 147. (7) Az-Zarkāshī (d. 794 AH), *al-Burhān*, p. 197. (8) Ibn Hājar al-Asqalānī (d. 852), *Fatḥ al-Barī Sharḥ Ṣaḥīḥ al-Bukhārī*, 7:104.

As for Shī'īte reference books of *ḥadīth*, refer to the following references:

(1) Al-Kulaynī (d. 328 AH), *Uṣūl al-Kāfī*, 1:287. (2) Ibn Babawayh (d. 329 AH), *al-Imāmah wa't-Tabṣirah*, p. 47, Ḥ. 29. (3) Al-Maghribī (d. 363 AH), *Da'ā'im al-Islām*, pp. 35, 37. (4) Aṣ-Ṣadūq (d. 381 AH), *al-Khiṣāl*, pp. 403, 550. (5) Aṭ-Ṭūsī (d. 460 AH), *al-Amālī*, Ḥ. 438, 482, 783.

For more details, refer to the exegesis of the holy verse involved in the following reference books of *tafsīr*: (1) Aṭ-Ṭabarī (d. 310 AH), *Book of Tafsīr*. (2) Al-Jassāss (d. 370 AH), *Aḥkām al-Qur'ān*. (3) Al-Waḥīdī (d. 468 AH), *Asbāb an-Nuzūl*. (4) Ibn al-Jawzī (d. 597 AH), *Zād al-Maṣīr*. (5) Al-Qurṭubī (d. 671 AH), *al-Jāmi' li-Aḥkām al-Qur'ān*. (6) Ibn Kathīr (d. 774 AH), *Book of Tafsīr*. (7) Ath-Tha'ālibī (d. 825 AH), *Book of Tafsīr*. (8) As-Suyūtī (d. 911 AH), *ad-Durr al-Manthūr*. (9) Ash-Shawkanī (d. 1250 AH), *Fatḥ al-Qadīr*. (10) Al-'Ayyāshī (d. 320 AH), *Book of Tafsīr*. (11) Al-Qummī (d. 329 AH), *Book of Tafsīr*. (12) Furṭ al-Kūfī (d. 352 AH), *Book of Tafsīr*; in the margin of the exegesis of verse 4:59. (13) At-Tabrisī (d. 560 AH), *Majma' al-Bayān*, as well as many other reference books of *ḥadīth* and *tafsīr*.

The Qur'an as Reflected in Nahj al-Balāghah

قَالَ رَسُولُ قَالَ رَسُولُ اللهِ:

إِنِّي تَارِكٌ فِيكُمُ الثَّقَلَيْنِ: كِتَابَ اللهِ وَعِتْرَتِي أَهْلَ بَيْتِي، مَا إِنْ تَمَسَّكْتُمْ بِهِمَا لَنْ تَضِلُّوا بَعْدِي أَبَداً، وَإِنَّهُمَا لَنْ يَفْتَرِقَا حَتَّى يَرِدَا عَلَيَّ الْحَوْضَ

The Messenger of Allah (*ṣ*) said:

"Verily, I am leaving among you two weighty things [thaqalayn]: The Book of Allah and my progeny ['itrat], the members of my Household [Ahl al-Bayt]. If you hold fast to them, you shall never go astray. These two will never separate from each other until they meet me at the Pond [*ḥ*aw*ḍ*] (of Kawthar)."

Some references:

- Al-Ḥākim al-Nayshābūrī, *Al-Mustadrak 'alā al-Ṣaḥīḥayn* (Beirut), vol. 3, pp. 109-110, 148, 533
- Muslim, *Al-Ṣaḥīḥ*, (English translation), book 31, *ḥadīth*s 5920-3
- Al-Tirmidhī, *Al-Ṣaḥīḥ*, vol. 5, pp. 621-2, *ḥadīth*s 3786, 3788; vol. 2, p. 219
- Al-Nasā'ī, *Khaṣā'iṣ 'Alī ibn Abī Ṭālib*, *ḥadīth* 79
- Aḥmad ibn Ḥanbal, *Al-Musnad*, vol. 3, pp. 14, 17, 26; vol. 3, pp. 26, 59; vol. 4, p. 371; vol. 5, pp. 181-182, 189-190
- Ibn al-'Athīr, *Jāmi' al-Uṣūl*, vol. 1, p. 277
- Ibn Kathīr, *Al-Bidāyah wa al-Nihāyah*, vol. 5, p. 209
- Ibn Kathīr, *Tafsīr al-Qur'ān al-'Aẓīm* , vol. 6, p. 199
- Naṣīr al-Dīn al-Albānī, *Silsilat al-Aḥādīth al-Ṣaḥīḥah* (Kuwait: Al-Dār al-Salafiyyah), vol. 4, pp. 355-358

THE QUR'AN

as Reflected in

NAHJ AL-BALĀGHAH

Professor Muḥammad Taqī Miṣbāḥ Yazdī

Translator

Mansoor Limba

Cultural Affairs Department

Ahl al-Bayt[('a)] World Assembly

نام کتاب: قرآن در آیینه نهج البلاغه
نویسنده: استاد محمّد تقی مصباح یزدی
مترجم: منصور لیمبا
زبان ترجمه: انگلیسی

***Title*: The Qur'an as Reflected in Nahj al-Balāghah**
Author: Professor Muḥammad Taqī Miṣbāḥ Yazdī
Translator and typesetter: Mansoor Limba
Project supervisor: Translation Unit, Cultural Affairs Department
Ahl al-Bayt (*'a*) World Assembly (ABWA)
Editor: Iffat Shah
Proofreader: Majid Karimi
Publisher: ABWA Publishing and Printing Center
First Printing: 2010
Printed by :Mojab Press
Copies: 5,000
ISBN: 978-964-529-572-9

---

www.ahl-ul-bait.org
info@ahl-ul-bayt.org

Table of Contents

Transliteration Symbols

Symbol	Transliteration	Symbol	Transliteration
ء	’	أ	a
ب	B	ت	t
ث	th	ج	j
ح	ḥ	خ	kh
د	D	ذ	dh
ر	R	ز	z
س	S	ش	sh
ص	ṣ	ض	ḍ
ط	ṭ	ظ	ẓ
ع	‘	غ	gh
ف	F	ق	q
ك	K	ل	l
م	M	ن	n
هـ	H	و	w
ي	Y	ة	ah
Long Vowels		**Short Vowels**	
آ	Ā	ـَ	a
اي	Ī	ـِ	i
او	Ū	ـُ	u
Persian Letters			
Symbol	**Transliteration**	**Symbol**	**Transliteration**
پ	P	چ	ch
ژ	Zh	گ	g

Preface

In the Name of Allah, the All-beneficent, the All-merciful

The preservation of the precious legacy left behind by the Holy Prophet's Household [*ahl al-bayt*] (may peace be upon them all) by their followers from the menace of extinction is exemplified by an all-encompassing school [*maktab*], which covers all the different branches of Islamic knowledge and trains sincere seekers of the truth. It has on its list of scholars many talented personalities who have benefited from this immense wealth of knowledge. This school has presented scholars to the Muslim *ummah* who, by following the Holy Prophet's Household (*'a*), have been granted the authority to remove doubts and skepticism encountered by various creeds and intellectual trends both inside and outside the Muslim society, and have throughout the past centuries, presented the firmest answers and solutions to these doubts.

Anchored in the responsibilities it is shouldering, the Ahl al-Bayt (*'a*) World Assembly has embarked upon defending the sanctity of *risālah* [apostleship] and its authentic beliefs—truths which have always been opposed by chiefs and leaders of anti-Islamic sects, religions and trends. The Assembly regards itself as a follower of the upright pupils of the *Ahl al-Bayt*'s (*'a*) school—those who have always, based on the expediencies of time and space, logically refuted all accusations and been foremost in their efforts to clarify all misunderstandings and misinterpretations.

The empirical knowledge preserved in their books (of the scholars of the *Ahl al-Bayt*'s (*'a*) school) is unique because it is based upon intellect and reasoning, devoid of any iota of blind prejudice, whims or caprice. It addresses experts, scholars and thinkers in a manner that is acceptable to a healthy human mind [*fiṭrah*].

In order to disseminate the truth, the Ahl al-Bayt (*'a*) World Assembly has included this valuable knowledge within the framework of research and writing of contemporary Shī'ah writers or those who, through divine guidance, embrace this noble school.

This Assembly is also engaged in the study and publication of valuable works of pious predecessors and outstanding Shī'ah personalities so that seekers of truth can quench their thirst from this refreshing fountain of knowledge offered by the Holy Prophet's Household (*'a*) as a gift to the entire world.

It is hoped that our readers do not deprive the Ahl al-Bayt (*'a*) World Assembly of their valuable views and suggestions as well as constructive criticism in this arena.

We also invite scholars, translators and other institutions to assist us in propagating the pure Muḥammadan Islam.

We ask God the Exalted, to accept this trivial effort and enhance it further under the auspices of His vicegerent on earth, Ḥaḍrat al-Mahdī (may Allah the Exalted, expedite his glorious advent).

We express our utmost gratitude to Professor Āyatullāh Muḥammad Taqī Miṣbāḥ Yazdī for writing the book, Mr. Mansoor Limba for translating it, and all our honorable colleagues, especially the dear ones in the Translation Office for accomplishing this task. /

Cultural Affairs Department
Ahl al-Bayt (*'a*) World Assembly

Introduction

In the Name of Allah, the All-beneficent, the All-merciful

اَلحَمدُ للهِ رَبِّ العالَمين

و صَلَّى اللهُ عَلىٰ سَيِّدِنَا وَ نَبِيِّنا مُحَمَّدٍ وَ آلِهِ الطّاهِرِينَ وَ لَعنَةُ اللهِ عَلىٰ اَعدائِهِم اَجمَعِينَ

All praise is due to Allah, the Lord of the worlds, and may the blessings of Allah be upon our Master and Prophet, Muhammad, and his pure progeny, and may the curse of Allah be upon all their enemies.

Although we believe that the Holy Qur'an is the greatest divine gift to mankind and the most precious legacy of the Holy Prophet (ṣ)[1] to the Muslims, the Muslim *ummah*[2] has not shown the requisite interest in using this precious legacy. Notwithstanding the repeated emphasis of the Apostle (ṣ) on the obligation to refer to and act upon the Qur'an as the greater of the two weighty things [*thiql al-akbar*] and to learn the sciences of the Qur'an from the *Ahl al-Bayt*[3] (*'a*)[1] as the great of the two weighty things [*thiql al-kabīr*],

1 The abbreviation, "ṣ", stands for the Arabic invocative phrase, *ṣallallāhu 'alayhi wa ālihī wa sallam* [may God's blessings and peace be upon him and his progeny], which is mentioned after the name of the Holy Prophet Muḥammad (ṣ). [Trans.]

2 *Ummah*; the entire Islamic community which knows no territorial, racial, national or ethnic distinction. [Trans.]

3 *Ahl al-Bayt*: according to authentic *ḥadīth*s recorded in both Sunnī and Shī'ah sources, the term *Ahl al-Bayt*, and interchangeably *'Itrah* and *Āl*, is a blessed Qur'anic appellation that belongs exclusively to the Prophet, 'Alī, Fāṭimah, Ḥasan, and Ḥusayn (*'a*). The members of this Family of five, with the Prophet Muḥammad (ṣ) at its head, were the ones alive at the time the Qur'anic verses regarding their virtues were being revealed to the Prophet (ṣ).

the Muslims neglected his advice of firmly clasping the unifying cord of Allah [*ḥabl Allāh*],[2] after his (*ṣ*) demise, and got divided into sects. Consequently, Muslim society lagged behind its original status which is described in the Qur'an in this manner: ﴿ وَأَنتُمُ الأَعْلَوْنَ إِن كُنتُم مُّؤْمِنِينَ ﴾ *"You shall have the upper hand, should you be truthful."*[3] Nowadays, one must acknowledge the painful reality that on account of drifting away from the reality of the Qur'an and the knowledge of the *Ahl al-Bayt* (*'a*), Muslim society has incurred irreparable losses.

In spite of drifting away from the reality of the Qur'an and being alienated from this heavenly gem and gift of the All-beneficent, outward heedfulness to it has gained momentum and remarkably increased among Muslims today.

All Muslims recognize the Qur'an as the sacred heavenly scripture revealed to the blessed Apostle (*ṣ*) on the Night of Ordainment [*laylat al-qadr*].[4] Now, printing the Holy Qur'an on high quality paper with golden covers, reading and memorizing it, mastering the sciences pertaining to its outward aspects such as correct pronunciation and recitation [*tajwīd*] have found a special place in the culture of Muslims. We occasionally witness annual competitions of recitation and memorization of the Holy Qur'an at the international level, and this itself has become a source of prosperity.

Of course, it must not remain unsaid that the ever-growing attention paid to the Holy Qur'an in other Muslim countries has been to some extent due to

---

However, nine other Imāms from the descendants of Imām al-Ḥusayn (*'a*) are also included in this chosen Family, the final one being Imām al-Mahdī (*'a*). For further information, visit: http://www.al-islam.org/faq. [Trans.]

1 The abbreviation, "*'a*" stands for the Arabic invocative phrase, *'alayhi's-salām*, *'alayhim'us-salām*, or *'alayhā's-salām* [may peace be upon him/them/her], which is mentioned after the names of the prophets, angels, Imāms from the Prophet's progeny, and saints (*'a*). [Trans.]

2 Sunnī scholars quoted Imām Ja'far al-Ṣādiq (*'a*), the sixth Imām from the Family of the Prophet [*Ahl al-Bayt*] (*'a*) as saying: "We are the Cord of Allah about whom Allah has said: *'Hold fast, all together, to Allah's cord, and do not be divided [into sects]'* (*Sūrah Āl 'Imrān* 3:103)." See Al-Tha'labī, *Tafsīr al-Kabīr*, under commentary of verse 3:103; Ibn Ḥajar al-Haythamī, *Al-Ṣawā'iq al-Muḥriqah* (Cairo), Ch. 11, section 1, p. 233. [Trans.]

3 *Sūrah Āl 'Imrān* 3:139. In this volume, the translation of Qur'anic passages is adapted from Sayyid 'Alī Qulī Qarā'ī, *The Qur'an with a Phrase-by-Phrase English Translation* (London: Islamic College for Advanced Studies Press, 2004). [Trans.]

4 *Sūrah al-Qadr* 97:1-5. [Trans.]

His Eminence Imām Khomeinī (*r*)[1] and the victory of the Islamic Revolution in Iran because it was after the message of the eminent Imām (*r*) to the administration of the Two Holy Places [*al-ḥaramayn al-sharīfayn*] (Mecca and Medina) conveyed by a council [*shawrā*] consisting of representatives from many Muslim countries, that Saudi Arabia undertook the reparation and development of the two holy sites along with the printing and distribution of copies of the Qur'an to the *Ḥajj* pilgrims from around the world, in order to present itself as the pioneer in propagating Islam and the Qur'an and undermine the attention paid by the Muslims to the Islamic Republic of Iran.

Focusing on the outward aspects of the Qur'an and keeping away from its truth has been one of the greatest problems owing to which Muslims have received severe blows. As long as Muslims do not move from the exoteric aspects of the Qur'an towards its esoteric aspects and transform empty rhetoric into practice, the guidance of the Qur'an will not be achieved by them.

This volume is not an attempt to examine the reasons behind the straying of the Muslims from the truth of the Qur'an and the Prophet's progeny [*'itrah*] (*'a*) after the passing away of the Holy Prophet (*ṣ*). It rather endeavors to present some dimensions of the truth of the Qur'an from the viewpoint of *Nahj al-Balāghah*[2] and the Holy Book itself, and to acquaint the readers with the Qur'an and its greatness from the perspective of the Commander of the Faithful (*'a*). It also deals with and addresses some misgivings expressed by certain enemies. In the concluding part, these misgivings are also mentioned through the sermons of 'Alī (*'a*)—the speaking [*nāṭiq*] Qur'an—and the factors and motives for expressing them.

The subjects of this book are actually the transcript of a series of lectures given by His Eminence Āyatullāh Miṣbāḥ Yazdī in Ramaḍān 1419-20 AH (December 21, 1998-January 18, 1999 and December 10, 1999-January 8,

---

1 The abbreviation, "*r*" stands for the Arabic invocative phrase, *raḥmatullāh 'alayhi*, *raḥmatullāh 'alayhā*, or *raḥmatullāh 'alayhim* [may peace be upon him/her/them], which is used after the names of pious people. [Trans.]

2 *Nahj al-Balāghah* (The Peak of Eloquence) is a collection of speeches, sayings and letters of the Commander of the Faithful, Imām 'Alī ibn Abī Ṭālib (*'a*) compiled by Sharīf al-Raḍī Muḥammad ibn al-Ḥusayn (d. 406 AH/1016). The contents of the book concern the three essential topics of God, man and the universe, and include comments on scientific, literary, social, ethical, and political issues. With the exception of the words of the Glorious Qur'an and of the Holy Prophet (*ṣ*), no words of man can equal it in eloquence. So far, more than 101 exegeses have been written on *Nahj al-Balāghah*, indicating the importance of this treatise to scholars and learned men of research and investigation. For more information, visit: http://www.al-islam.org/nahjul. [Trans.]

2000) in Qum. The subjects touched by Professor Yazdī are not abridged and disarranged but conversational language has been rendered closer to the written word, with an effort to maintain perfect or total accuracy in compiling and editing this book.

In conclusion, we are thankful to the erudite scholars, Ḥujjat al-Islām Aḥmad Muḥammadī for transcribing and compiling the topics of this book, and Ḥujjat al-Islām Muḥammad Mahdī Nādirī Qummī for editing it. We beseech the munificent God for their continued success. χ

Imām Khomeinī Educational and Research Institute

Chapter 1

The Status of the Qur'an in Religious Society

The Qur'an as the only heavenly book at the disposal of mankind

If we would like to deal with everything about the Qur'an mentioned in *Nahj al-Balāghah*, it will become a very long discussion. Imām 'Alī (*'a*) has introduced the Qur'an and its status in more than 20 sermons recorded in *Nahj al-Balāghah*. Sometimes, he (*'a*) has allocated more than half of a sermon in elucidating the status of the Qur'an, its role in the life of Muslims and their duty towards this heavenly book. Here, we shall only explain some of *Nahj al-Balāghah*'s descriptions of the Holy Qur'an.

The Imām (*'a*) says in Sermon 133:

وَكِتَابُ اللهِ بَيْنَ أَظْهُرِكُمْ، نَاطِقٌ لاَ يَعْيَا لِسَانُهُ.

> "The Book of Allah is among you. It speaks and its tongue does not falter."[1]

That is to say, "The Qur'an is accessible to you. Contrary to other heavenly scriptures like the ones revealed to Ḥaḍrat[2] Mūsā (Moses) and Ḥaḍrat 'Īsā (Jesus) ('a), the Qur'an is at your disposal." It is said that in the past, especially among the Jews, the revealed scripture had not been at the

---

1 In this volume, the translation of quotations from *Nahj al-Balāghah* is adapted from Syed 'Ali Raza, *Nahj al-Balāghah: The Peak of Eloquence* (Qum: Foundation of Islamic Cultural Propagation in the World, 1995). [Trans.]

2 *Ḥaḍrat*: The Arabic word *Ḥaḍrat* is used as a respectful form of address. [Trans.]

disposal of the masses. Only some parts of the Torah were at the disposal of Jewish divines and it was not possible for the masses to have access to it.

Regarding the heavenly scripture revealed to Ḥaḍrat 'Īsā ('a), its status has been more worrisome because what is known today as the Gospel [injīl] among the Christians is not the book revealed to Ḥaḍrat 'Īsā al-Masīḥ (Jesus the Messiah) ('a). It rather consists of subjects compiled by certain individuals and known as the Four Canonical Gospels.[1] Thus, former communities were deprived of access to the heavenly scriptures. But the Qur'an has a different story. The manner of revelation of the Qur'an and its reciting and teaching by the Holy Prophet (*ṣ*) was such that the people memorized its verses and the Qur'an in its complete form was at their disposal. Among the other important distinctions of this heavenly book is that God the Exalted Himself assumes the responsibility of guarding and preserving the Holy Qur'an from any form of threat. In addition, the Messenger of Allah (*ṣ*) made sure the Muslims memorized its divine verses so that a good number of Muslims had memorized the whole Qur'an within his lifetime. They used to prepare manuscripts of verses as soon as they were revealed and gradually memorize them. The duplication of these manuscripts and learning of the Qur'an by heart made it accessible to everybody.

Ḥaḍrat 'Alī ('a) says: "The Book of Allah is among you. It speaks and its tongue does not falter." It is worthy to reflect on the second statement. That is to say, this book has the power of speech and its tongue neither falters nor feels tired. He ('a) continues:

وَبَيْتٌ لاَ تُهْدَمُ أَرْكَانُهُ، وَعِزٌّ لاَ تُهْزَمُ أَعْوَانُهُ.

> "It is a house whose pillars do not fall down, and a power whose supporters are never routed."

The Qur'anic mode of speech

On one hand, in describing the Qur'an in *Nahj al-Balāghah* Imām 'Alī (*'a*) says that this book is a talking book and is not tired of speaking. It clearly expresses itself. On the other hand, the Imām (*'a*) says this Qur'an does not speak. It must be induced to speak and "I am the one who expounds this Qur'an to you." In some instances, he (*'a*) described the Qur'an as a "silent

1 That is, the first four books of the New Testament, viz. the Gospels of Mark, Luke, Matthew, and John. [Trans.]

speaker" [*ṣāmitun nāṭiq*].[1] The Qur'an is a speaker, but a silent one. What does that mean?

It seems that this expression points to two different perspectives on this heavenly book. One perspective holds that the Qur'an is a sacred but silent book placed in a corner. It does not talk to anyone and no one communicates with it. The second perspective is that it is a talking book which addresses all human beings, calls on them to follow its guidance, and gives glad tidings of success and deliverance to its followers.

Obviously, the Qur'an, whose only description is sacredness, consists of words, statements and verses written on paper. The Muslims kiss and show respect to it and place it in the best part of their homes. Sometimes, they recite it in gatherings without paying attention to its meaning. If we view the Qur'an in this manner, then it is a silent book which does not produce a specific sound. Anyone who has such a view of the Qur'an will never hear a word from it and the Holy Qur'an will never solve any of his problems.

Therefore, we are duty-bound to follow the second perspective. That is, we have to regard the Qur'an as the book of life. By cultivating the spirit of submission to God, the Exalted, we have to be prepared to listen to the message of the Holy Qur'an which contains instructions for a better life. It is in this way that the Qur'an speaks and articulates, talking to human beings and guiding them in all aspects of life.

In addition to this interpretation of the Qur'an as "a silent speaker" which we mentioned, there is a deeper meaning of it which is what Ḥaḍrat 'Alī (*'a*) refers to when he says, "I am the one who expounds this Qur'an to you."

It is true that the Holy Qur'an is the Word of God, the Exalted, and the truth of this divine word and the manner of its revelation are beyond our comprehension but since the purpose is the guidance of mankind, this Word of God is simplified in the form of words, statements and verses that can be read and heard by all human beings. Yet, it is not correct to say that the contents of all verses can be grasped and comprehended by the average mind and the meaning of the verses understood without referring to the interpretation and explanation of the Apostle (*ṣ*), the infallible Imāms ('a) and those well grounded in knowledge.

For instance, details and explanations of the particular aspects of law are not mentioned in the Qur'an. Moreover, verses of the Holy Qur'an are concise, and thus, they are in need of explanation and elucidation. Therefore, for

1 *Nahj al-Balāghah*, Sermon 147. It must be noted that throughout this book all citations from *Nahj al-Balāghah* are based upon Fayḍ al-Islām Arrangement.

many reasons the Qur'an is "silent" [*ṣāmit*]. That is, in the absence of the explanation and interpretation of one who has divine knowledge and awareness, it is of no use for the commoner.

The Apostle (ṣ) and explanation of the Qur'an

One of the responsibilities of the Apostle (*ṣ*) to the *ummah* is to expound the divine verses. Addressing the Apostle (*ṣ*), the Holy Qur'an states:

﴿ وَأَنزَلْنَا إِلَيْكَ الذِّكْرَ لِتُبَيِّنَ لِلنَّاسِ مَا نُزِّلَ إِلَيْهِمْ ﴾

> *"We have sent down the reminder to you so that you may clarify for the people that which has been sent down to them."*[1]

The Qur'an is God's Word and although it has been much reduced to become words and verses at the disposal of the Muslims, its profound gnosis cannot be comprehended by a layman. It is for this reason that the Qur'an is "silent" for the commoners and is in need of the interpretation and explanation of the Apostle (*ṣ*) and infallible Imāms (*'a*) because the verses of the Qur'an have specific interpretations which are known only to the Apostle (*ṣ*) and infallible Imāms (*'a*) who imparted the sciences of the Qur'an to the Muslims and conveyed its message to the people. It must be noted, however, that the Qur'an declares its message whether it is pleasant or unpleasant to the addressee. Sometimes, it is consistent with what he likes, and at times, it is contrary to the carnal desires of man. The devils among men have no right to impose whims upon the Qur'an, and in the name of personal understanding of the Qur'an, speculatively interpret God's Word. We shall elaborate on this in the future.

According to the two stated meanings of the Qur'an being "a silent speaker," Ḥaḍrat 'Alī (*'a*) conveys its message to the people and provides the proof [*ḥ*ujjah] to the Muslims.

In describing the Holy Qur'an in Sermon 157, the Commander of the Faithful ('a) thus says:

ذلِكَ الْقُرْآنُ فَاسْتَنْطِقُوهُ، وَلَنْ يَنْطِقَ، وَلكِنْ أُخْبِرُكُمْ عَنْهُ أَلاَ إِنَّ فِيهِ عِلْمَ مَا يَأْتِي، وَالْحَدِيثَ عَنِ الْمَاضِي، وَدَوَاءَ دَائِكُمْ، وَنَظْمَ مَا بَيْنَكُمْ.

> "It is the Qur'an. If you ask it to speak it won't do so; but I will tell you about it. Know that it contains knowledge of what is to come about, stories of the past, cure for your ills and regulation for whatever faces you."

1 *Sūrah al-Naḥl* 16:44.

The Qur'an is an ocean of divine knowledge and learning. Only those who have connection with the unseen world can dive into its unfathomable depth and acquire its man-perfecting pearls. God, the Exalted, has also urged the people to acquire the lofty knowledge of the Qur'an under the aegis of the grace, knowledge, assistance, and instructions of the Apostle (*ṣ*) and the Imāms of guidance (*'a*) because the sciences of the Qur'an are with the *Ahl al-Bayt* (*'a*). As such, their words are those of the Qur'an. For this reason, the Apostle (ṣ) and infallible Imāms ('a) are called "the talking Qur'an" [*qur'ān nāṭiq*].

In accordance with the abovementioned basis, Ḥaḍrat 'Alī (*'a*) says: "It is the Qur'an. If you ask it to speak it won't do so." That is, "This is the Qur'an and here you are. As you can see, without the explanation of the infallible Imāms (*'a*) you cannot make use of the Qur'an! These infallible Imāms (*'a*) are supposed to interpret and explain the Qur'an to you and teach you the knowledge and sciences of the Qur'an.

After these preliminary remarks, the Commander of the Faithful (*'a*) approaches the Qur'an through another angle, calling on the people to refer to and reflect upon the Qur'an. That is to say, the infallible Imām is supposed to impart the knowledge and sciences of the Qur'an to the Muslims, and the Qur'an by itself cannot talk whereas the people are incapable of directly grasping the divine messages. The Imām (*'a*) then says: "But I will tell you about it." That is to say, "I will inform you of the Qur'an and teach you the knowledge and sciences pertaining to it, so that you know that everything you need is in the Holy Qur'an: 'Know that it contains knowledge of what is to come about, stories of the past, cure for your ills and regulation for whatever faces you'." That is, "It is you who must settle your affairs by referring to the Holy Qur'an and the knowledge of the *Ahl al-Bayt* (*'a*)."

Mentioning two points

First, the Qur'an is the most important historical document for the Muslims and followers of this heavenly book. Since the Qur'an mentions historical events and says something about the thoughts and beliefs of past nations and communities as well as their way of life and destinies, it is the most credible historical document. In comparison to historical books and scripts devoid of Qur'anic attestation, even if they are reported with the complete chain of transmission, their value or credibility does not exceed that of the Qur'an. Thus, stories of prophets (*'a*) and past communities must be heard from the Qur'an and lessons learned from them.

By referring to the Qur'an and studying the life accounts of past communities and nations we must learn our lessons and set our lives on the path of truth.

Secondly, the Holy Qur'an also gives information about the future. Obviously, to talk scientifically and accurately about the future could be done only by God, the Exalted, and those who are informed of the future by His decree. It is God for whom the past, present or future has no meaning and who can talk and give information about the future. It is God who can clearly show the way to His servants and teach them how to behave in order to attain success. It is the Holy Qur'an that gives information about the past and future and makes the people aware of them. Hence, Imām 'Alī (*'a*) says: "Know that it contains knowledge of what is to come about and stories of the past."

The role of the Qur'an in life

Ḥaḍrat 'Alī (*'a*) presented the Qur'an as the panacea to all problems: "It contains a cure for your ills and regulations for whatever faces you." The Qur'an's existence treats all pains and agonies. This medical prescription must be read and studied carefully, and one must be familiar with the way of curing individuals and social ills and predicaments.

Evidently, before experiencing and identifying the pain or problem, it is abnormal to talk about the cure because the individual and social ills must initially be identified and one must be acquainted with them by thoroughly studying the noble verses of the Qur'an. Then, by acting upon this medical prescription one must treat them. Today, there are many problems—individual and social—in our society and everybody wants to get rid of them. Notwithstanding the astounding advancements in different fields of endeavor, still many problems remain unsolved and the concerned authorities are trying to solve them in one way or another.

In Sermon 189, he (*'a*) says with a slight variation: "[It is] a cure after which there is no ailment."

The point which must be heeded before anything else is faith in the statement of Ḥaḍrat 'Alī (*'a*). That is, we have to sincerely believe that the real cure to our individual and social ills and problems is in the Qur'an. We all acknowledge this fact but people have different degrees of faith [*īmān*] and certainty [*yaqīn*]. It is true that there are individuals who sincerely believe that if they refer to the Qur'an and act upon its knowledge and instructions, it will prove to be the best medical prescription for all ailments. Yet, such people are very few and perhaps one of the most serious problems of our society is the weakness of faith in this respect, and this is the reason why many problems remain unsolved. Some individuals may possibly question: "In spite of the fact that the Qur'an is at our disposal and we claim to follow it, why are our problems still unsolved and the people are still suffering from economic problems like inflation, overpricing and thousands of social and individual, moral and cultural problems?" Let us reply to this question.

The Qur'an as the universal source of guidance

The Qur'an is concerned with the eternal destiny of man and it aims for his deliverance and salvation in this world and the hereafter. The Holy Qur'an shows us the highways and main roads by treading which we can have a blissful life. These general ways are beacons that direct actions and movements. It must be noted, however, that in attaining salvation and felicity in this world and the hereafter, solving problems, and establishing a progressive and at the same time Islamic or religious society, God, the Exalted, has endowed man with two means, viz. religion [*dīn*] and intellect [*'aql*].

The Qur'an presents the highways of human progress and perfection, and an Islamic society is duty-bound to pave the ground for the realization of the lofty goals of the Qur'an by using the human intellect and scientific experience. The Qur'an regards knowledge as a divine asset and urges Muslims to acquire it from wherever and whoever they can, irrespective of whether it be a Muslim or non-Muslim. The Apostle (*ṣ*) urged Muslims to gain knowledge in various fields of study:

أُطْلُبُوا ٱلْعِلْمَ وَلَوْ بِالصِّين .

"Seek knowledge even if it be in China."[1]

That is to say, "Seek knowledge and make use of the scientific experiences of others even if it requires traveling long distances." Nowadays, international relations are complex, and, by using the products of scientific experiments, the arrogant countries and economic powers want to strengthen their hegemonic relations. Yet, with utmost sagacity and without making the least compromise in the pursuit of our Islamic and Qur'anic objectives, we have to make use of the scientific achievements of man in various fields to improve our economic conditions and solve the daily problems of people.

Therefore, the Qur'an is not meant to address all the big and small problems in the life of man. It rather states the basic ways of achieving felicity and

1 *Biḥār al-Anwār*, vol. 1, p. 177.

perfection, and calls Muslims towards them. In line with the statement of Ḥaḍrat 'Alī (*'a*) about the healing power of the Qur'an, we shall point out one of the general ways implied by the Qur'an and explain it as a sample.

An example of the general ways of the Qur'an

The Holy Qur'an states:

﴿ وَلَوْ أَنَّ أَهْلَ الْقُرَى آمَنُوا وَاتَّقَوا لَفَتَحْنَا عَلَيْهِم بَرَكَاتٍ مِّنَ السَّمَاء وَالأَرْضِ وَلَـكِن كَذَّبُواْ فَأَخَذْنَاهُم بِمَا كَانُوا يَكْسِبُونَ ﴾

> *"If the people of the towns had been faithful and God-wary, We would have opened to them blessings from the heavens and the earth. But they denied; so We seized them because of what they used to earn."*[1]

This is one of the precise verses [*muḥkamāt*] of the Qur'an in which there is nothing allegorical. Its meaning is clear and unambiguous. There is no doubt in it, and in this linguistic frame only one interpretation can be inferred by those who know Arabic.

This verse contains one of the general ideological guidelines and at the same time indicates a means of solving economic problems and difficulties in life. The noble verse explains with utmost clarity that economic development and progress in the life of the faithful, removal of economic hardships, sending down of divine grace, and in general, opening of blessings from the heavens and the earth lie on faith [*īmān*] and God-wariness [*taqwā*]. In contrast, it considers ungratefulness and denial of the divine favors as causing the withholding of blessings and the sending down of calamities and different types of problems. It regards gratitude and appreciation of the favors as the cause of more favors and the denial of them as inviting wrath. The Qur'an says:

﴿ لَئِن شَكَرْتُمْ لأَزِيدَنَّكُمْ وَلَئِن كَفَرْتُمْ إِنَّ عَذَابِي لَشَدِيدٌ ﴾

> *"If you are grateful, I will surely enhance you [in blessing], but if you are ungrateful, My punishment is indeed severe."*[2]

Here, I shall point to one of the great divine blessings bestowed on the great nation of Iran on account of following the Holy Qur'an. We pray to God to grant the people the ability to give thanks for it and we seek refuge in the

---

1 *Sūrah al-A'rāf* 7:96.

2 *Sūrah Ibrāhīm* 14:7.

Sacred Essence of God from the withdrawal from us of this great blessing on account of ingratitude.

Manifestation of divine grace in the establishment of the Islamic government

We all acknowledge that after the martyrdom of Imām 'Alī (*'a*), the greatest wish of us Muslims has been the establishment of a just government based upon divine revelation and ordinances. For many long years, our forebears and ancestors had been praying for the establishment of such a government. While living under the yoke and dominance of tyrants and monarchs and having no significant role in administering their social affairs, the establishment of the Islamic government seemed to be an idealistic, unrealizable and impossible affair.

After almost fourteen centuries, due to the Muslims' resorting to the Holy Qur'an and the leadership of the *walī al-faqīh* [jurist-guardian] and deputy of the infallible Imām (*'a*), God, the Exalted, granted one of His greatest blessings, i.e. the Islamic government to the people of Iran at this point in history. Obviously, we do not intend to account for the defects and shortcomings or justify outputs. Rather, what we want to emphasize is that the establishment of this sacred system with the aim of implementing the divine decrees is one of the divine graces.

Now, twenty years[1] after the victory of the Islamic Revolution, what has been the cause of concern and anxiety of the supporters of the Revolution and guardians of the religious and moral values is the loss of faith and God-wariness in society and the gradual diminishing of the religious and revolutionary values. As a result, the enemies of Islam and Iran might succeed in executing their plans of cultural onslaught and invasion and again dominate the Muslim people of Iran by alienating the people, especially the youth, from the religious and revolutionary values.

At this juncture, this question may possibly be asked: What must be done so that the ideological and religious values of society can be preserved, the enemies fail in executing their plans, and we overcome all our problems?

Ḥaḍrat 'Alī (*'a*) also pays attention to this point in Sermon 157 of *Nahj al-Balāghah* and presents resorting to the Qur'an and acting upon its commands as the way of solving individual and social problems.

1 Now, it is almost thirty years.

The solution to social problems lies in following the Qur'an

The statement of Ḥaḍrat 'Alī (*'a*) in this regard is a paraphrase of the eternally precious statement of the Holy Prophet of Islam (*ṣ*) who said:

إِذَا الْتَبَسَتْ عَلَيْكُمُ الْفِتَنُ كَقِطَعِ اللَّيْلِ الْمُظْلِمِ فَعَلَيْكُمْ بِالْقُرْآنِ.

> "Whenever agitation, worries, problems, instabilities, and seditions cast a shadow upon your society like the dark night and you make no progress in solving problems, you ought to refer to the Qur'an and set its salvation-giving guidelines as the basis of your actions."[1]

The hope-giving injunctions of the Qur'an revive the spirit of hope, victory against all odds, salvation, prosperity in the hearts, and deliver human beings from hopelessness and despair.

Obviously, every victory depends on the will and efforts of human beings. Therefore, if we want to keep our independence, freedom and Islamic government safe from any form of conspiracy under the protection of God, the Exalted, there is no option but to return to God and the salvation-giving decrees of the Qur'an, and repent on account of the ingratitude and profanities of xenomaniacs[2] [*gharbzadeh-hā*] for religious values.

It is naïve for us to think that the Global Arrogance would assist the officials of the Islamic Republic of Iran in issues that are beneficial to the Muslim nation of Iran and not consistent with their hegemonic interests. It is also an extreme act of ingratitude for us to abandon the Qur'an—this everlasting miracle [*mu'jizah*] of the Apostle (*ṣ*) and guarantor of felicity and salvation—and seek the help of enemies to solve our problems, and to discard *wilāyah al-faqīh* [guardianship of the jurist] which is the extension of the *wilāyah* of the Apostle (*ṣ*) and infallible Imāms (*'a*) and accept the guardianship and hegemony of the enemies of God. One must seek refuge in God from the day when the Muslim nation of Iran would incur the divine wrath due to ungratefulness for the great blessing of independence, honor and security, and pave the way for its own downfall and disgrace.

---

1 *Biḥār al-Anwār*, vol. 92, p. 17.

2 Xenomaniacs: those infatuated with foreign and especially Western models of culture. This is the translation of a Persian term, *gharbzadegān* or *gharbzadeh-hā*, popularized by Jalāl Āl Aḥmad (d. 1969) who was a writer of great influence in his book *Gharbzadegī* ("Xenomania" or "Occidentosis"). See its English translation, R. Campbell (trans.) and Hamid Algar (ed. and anno.), *Occidentosis: A Plague from the West* (Berkeley: Al-Mizan Press, 1984). [Trans.]

In any case, it is the duty of each member of the nation especially those who are in charge of the cultural affairs of the country to guard the sphere of beliefs and religious-moral values of society.

Those who do not have sufficient knowledge of religion and are under the influence of individualistic ideas and secular tendencies regarding the statement of Ḥaḍrat 'Alī (*'a*) think that it refers only to the spiritual and moral problems of the people. In our opinion, however, this notion is wrong because the subject of discussion includes both individual and social problems and maladies. By stating and expounding the statement of the Imām (*'a*), the groundlessness of the notion of separation of religion and politics and the falsity of secularism will become clear.

Organizing social affairs according to the guidelines of the Qur'an

Ḥaḍrat 'Alī (*'a*) says:

أَلاَ إِنَّ فِيهِ عِلْمَ مَا يَأْتِي، وَالْحَدِيثَ عَنِ الْمَاضِي، وَدَوَاءَ دَائِكُمْ، وَنَظْمَ مَا بَيْنَكُمْ.

> "Know that it contains knowledge of what is to come about, stories of the past, cure for your ills and regulation for whatever faces you."[1]

After stating that the Qur'an contains knowledge of the past and the future and it is the panacea to all ailments, the Imām (*'a*) mentions this point: "... and regulation for whatever faces you." That is to say, "The system or way of setting right your affairs is in the Qur'an. This heavenly book determines your social relations." In explaining this short statement we have no option but to make short preliminary remarks.

The greatest objective of every sociopolitical system is the maintenance of social order and security. There is no political school of thought in the world that rejects such an objective. In fact, the maintenance of order and security is among the principal duties of every government. It can also be said that the establishment of sociopolitical order is among the objectives of political science just as each political system dominant in the world declares it, at least in its slogan and propaganda, as one of its main objectives.

The role of an objective in social life

At this point, the role of an objective in social life must also be mentioned, for without it one cannot talk about social order. It is the objective that logically dictates certain actions. By doing certain actions in social life, individuals want to achieve that objective. In a sense, the objective also

1 *Nahj al-Balāghah*, Sermon 157.

originates from society since every society affirms a specific social order according to its primordial state in line with its culture and thought. Thus, in line with their hegemonic policies, the imperial powers strive to impel nations toward their imperialistic aims, make these nations alien to their original culture and control their culture and social order by imposing an imported culture.

Therefore, it must be seen what social order and the dominant culture and thought in society affirms. Obviously, the religious culture that originated from the Qur'an and monotheistic worldview affirms the social order which maintains the realization of the purpose of creation and the assurance of man's felicity and salvation in this world and the hereafter; and what is essentially the concern of Islam and the Qur'an is the salvation and perfection of man.

It is indeed lamentable that some "intellectuals" and liberals who are Muslims but do not have sufficient knowledge of the sociopolitical precepts of Islam and hardly have any religious concerns are unaware of this basic point. Whenever they talk about social order, they refer to the social order derived from Western democracy, and this Western social order stems from their secular thought. On account of their poor knowledge of religion, these "intellectuals" think that to organize the social affairs and systematically administer society is only possible through the separation of politics and religion. This itself is a product of cultural imperialism and regarded among the successes of the arrogant powers which, by stupefying the minds of the so-called intellectuals of the Third World countries, have been able to alienate them from their religious thought and turn them into promoters of the imperialist culture.

In any case, in the Islamic or monotheistic culture, everything including the social order is evaluated according to the purpose of creation. Obviously, the objective of social order in the religious or Qur'anic culture is not only to guarantee material welfare and worldly interests. Rather, the perfection of man and his success in the hereafter is also taken into account. It is clear that in case of conflict, success in the hereafter takes precedence over worldly affairs.

Now, by taking this introduction into account, we shall review and closely examine the statement of Ḥaḍrat 'Alī (*'a*) about the role of the Qur'an in securing the sociopolitical order of society so as to become more familiar with the viewpoint of *wilāyah* regarding the role and station of the Qur'an in social life.

By using an astounding expression, Ḥaḍrat 'Alī (*'a*) mentions the role of the Qur'an in organizing the social affairs of society and calls our attention to it lest we forgot it. After saying that the Qur'an is "the cure for your ills," the Imām (*'a*) says: "[The Qur'an contains] regulations for whatever faces you." That is to say, "The system of your affairs and relations is in the Qur'an." In other words, "If you are looking for the desirable and rational system under whose auspices all members of society can enjoy their legitimate rights, you have to regulate your affairs according to the instructions of the Qur'an."

It is no secret to those who are informed that the phrase "... and regulation for whatever faces you" refers to the social affairs and relations of individuals. It is true that every individual is duty-bound to organize his personal and private affairs according to the instructions of the Qur'an but the phrase "... and regulation for whatever faces you" does not encompass the personal affairs of individuals. As it is clear to those who know Arabic that in the statement under discussion Ḥaḍrat 'Alī ('a) wants to state the social dimensions of the Holy Qur'an.

By saying, "Your social order is in the Holy Qur'an," Imām 'Alī ('a) wants to tell the Muslims and his followers that they must organize their political affairs and social relations according to the Qur'an.

Of course, it is clear that as long as these stated admonitions are considered non-binding moral admonitions by the officials of the Islamic system and are not heartily accepted and believed by them, this heavenly healing prescription will not cure any of the social ills of our society. By mentioning the key points of the policy of the religious system, Imām 'Alī ('a) reveals the truths without acting upon which it is impossible to realize a human society based upon justice and equity, in which all individuals enjoy their rights and attain desirable perfection.

Therefore, the most fundamental and pivotal factor is the faith, belief or conviction of the government officials and authorities in the overall dictum and precepts of the Holy Qur'an. So long as they do not have sincere faith and firm conviction in the Qur'an and the efficiency of its instructions in solving the problems of society and ensuring the happiness of man, not only they do not take the Qur'an as a model in practice, but they also do not want to understand the Qur'an. Of course, since they rule over Muslim people in an Islamic country, in slogan they might ostensibly call themselves and their government an Islamic government just to preserve their standing in the eyes of their own people and other Muslims. This is while the only government model not discussed by them is the government based on the laws of Islam and patterned after the Qur'an. Yet, this alienation of so-called Islamic states from the religion and Qur'anic culture especially in relation to politics and the administration of society is something not unknown to the Muslims because they know that the systems of government in their respective countries are not Islamic and the dominant culture and mindset of the government officials are totally different from the mindset and paradigm based upon the Qur'anic culture.

What is astonishing and surprising for man and at the same time a cause of concern and regret is the cultural condition prevailing in our dear Islamic country of Iran—the country where a revolution based on the instructions of the Qur'an and the religious culture and under the leadership of the wilāyah al-faqīh has been successfully staged. It is indeed a pity and a cause of concern that the statements, stances and actions of some cultural officials show that they do not have sufficient knowledge of this heavenly book and do not regard the efficiency of the government paradigm derived from it as more than any Eastern or Western paradigm. They consistently move away from the principles of the Islamic Revolution and religious values. Owing to their lack of strong faith and true belief, implicitly or explicitly, they shamelessly express that the age of sovereignty of the Qur'an and the utility of religious culture in the realm of governance has passed and today human society is not in need of divine revelation as it can independently present better ways of administering society and maintaining order and security. It is appropriate at this juncture to point out the oppressive nature of the existing systems of government in the world and the tragedies and crimes perpetrated against nations in the name of advanced and civilized systems so as to expose more than ever the groundlessness of the said notion and the faithlessness and self-defeatism of its proponents. However, in order not to digress from the main topic and avoid prolonging the discussion, we shall not mention the existing injustices, violations of human rights, oppressions, crimes, and insecurities in man-made systems and we shall refer to the relevant references.

It is obvious that the utility of the government based on the instructions of the Qur'an in maintaining justice, equity and order in society will appear provided that the government officials and authorities believe in it, and actually observe the laws and ordinances of the Qur'an. Unless it is such, the Qur'an cannot rule over society. Therefore, the rule of the Qur'an in society depends on the true faith and belief of government officials in this heavenly book, which depends on their knowledge of this divine healing prescription and realizing the need for religion and divine government. Also, this feeling will not be attained except by generating the spirit of servitude to God and getting rid of the sense of arrogance and megalomania vis-à-vis the sovereignty of God, the Exalted. This sense of arrogance is the same sense of ingratitude that dismissed Satan from the station of proximity to the angelic station and nearness to God and subjected him to eternal perdition.

At this point, it is appropriate for us to pay heed to the discourse of Ḥaḍrat 'Alī (*'a*) in Sermon 175 of *Nahj al-Balāghah* that mentions the unpleasant consequences of drifting away from the Holy Qur'an. This discourse is a warning to those who, on one hand, present themselves as followers of 'Alī (*'a*), and on the other, regard the Qur'an and the model of government derived from it as insufficient for the administration of human society today and prefer defective human systems of government to the Qur'anic *wilāyah*. It is hoped that in the light of such instructions all members of our society particularly the decision-makers and government officials have stronger faith in the centrality of the Qur'an in Islamic society, and sincerely put its instructions into practice.

Self-sufficiency lies in following the Qur'an

In the said sermon, Ḥaḍrat 'Alī (*'a*) describes the Holy Qur'an as an indicator, saying:

> وَاعْلَمُوا أَنَّ هذَا الْقُرْآنَ هُوَ النَّاصِحُ الَّذِي لاَ يَغُشُّ، وَالْهَادِي الَّذِي لاَ يُضِلُّ، وَالْمحَدِّثُ الَّذِي لاَ يَكْذِبُ، وَمَا جَالَسَ هذَا الْقُرْآنَ أَحَدٌ إِلاَّ قَامَ عَنْهُ بِزِيَادَة أَوْ نُقْصَان زِيَادَة فِي هُدىً، أَوْ نُقْصَان مِنْ عَمىً
>
> "And know that this Qur'an is indeed an adviser who never deceives, a leader who never misleads, and a narrator who never speaks a lie. No one will sit beside this Qur'an but that when he rises he will achieve one addition or one diminution—addition in his guidance or elimination in his (spiritual) blindness."[1]

Then, Imām 'Alī (*'a*) says:

> وَاعْلَمُوا أَنَّهُ لَيْسَ عَلَى أَحَد بَعْدَ الْقُرْآنِ مِنْ فَاقَة، وَلاَ لاحَد قَبْلَ الْقُرْآنِ مِنْ غِنىً، فَاسْتَشْفُوهُ مِنْ أَدْوَائِكُمْ، وَاسْتَعِينُوا بِهِ عَلَى لاْوَائِكُمْ، فَإِنَّ فِيهِ شِفَاءً مِنْ أَكْبَرِ الدَّاءِ، وَهُوَ الْكُفْرُ وَالنِّفَاقُ، وَالْغَيُّ وَالضَّلاَلُ
>
> "You should also know that no one will need anything after (guidance from) the Qur'an and no one will be free from want before (guidance from) the Qur'an. Therefore, seek a cure from it for your ailments and seek its assistance in your distresses. It

---

1 *Nahj al-Balāghah*, Sermon 175.

> contains a cure for the biggest diseases, namely unbelief, hypocrisy, revolt and misguidance."[1]

That is, with the existence of the Qur'an and its rule over society, no need will remain unsolved for anyone because the Holy Qur'an is the most sublime divine program for the lives of the monotheists, and God, the Exalted, has guaranteed honor in this world and salvation in the hereafter for the followers of this heavenly book. Therefore, should our Islamic society abide by the revitalizing commands and instructions of the Qur'an and take it as their pattern of behavior by having faith in the truthfulness of its promises, it will solve individual and social, material and spiritual needs of society and make Islamic society needless of anything and anyone.

On the contrary, the Imām (*'a*) points out the peril of parting from the Qur'an. He rejects the notion that without the Qur'an—the greater one of the two weighty things [*thiql al-akbar*]—one can solve individual and social problems of society, and says: "No one will be free from want before (guidance from) the Qur'an [and the society will never be needless of the Qur'an." That is, in forming a society based on justice and equity and other moral values, even if all human learning and experiences are put into use and all ideas and thoughts are applied, in the absence of the Qur'an one will lead to nowhere. It is because without the Qur'an it is impossible for one to become independent and self-sufficient. As such, the Imām (*'a*) says: "Therefore, seek a cure from it for your ailments and seek its assistance in your distress." Then, by mentioning the most serious individual and social ailments and maladies—that is, unbelief, hypocrisy and misguidance—he says that the means of curing these ailments and maladies lies in the Qur'an and one can cure his ailments and maladies by referring to it.

Therefore, the general principles and main ways must be learned from the Qur'an, and problems solved by following those general principles and benefiting from experiences, reflection and thinking. If we intend to solve problems with this frame of mind, we will definitely overcome all odds in all aspects, for this is the divine promise. God, the Exalted, says:

﴿ وَمَن يَتَّقِ اللَّهَ يَجْعَل لَّهُ مَخْرَجًا ﴾

"And whoever is wary of Allah, He shall make a way out for him"[2]

---

1 *Ibid.*

2 *Sūrah* al-*Ṭalāq* 65:2.

The Qur'an as a panacea for the most serious maladies

The said statement will not be palatable to the arrogant and those whose faith in God is weak, whose knowledge of the Qur'an and the *Ahl al-Bayt* (*'a*) is insufficient, who think themselves equal to God merely because they possess some knowledge of the human sciences. Yet, every rational person admits that in comparison to his ignorance, all the astounding scientific advancements of man are but a drop vis-à-vis an ocean, and all the claims of atheistic moral philosophies in presenting the model of a virtuous city are nothing compared to the infinite divine knowledge of the sciences possessed by the *Ahl al-Bayt* (*'a*) that emanated from divine inspiration.

Ḥaḍrat 'Alī (*'a*) regards disbelief [*kufr*], hypocrisy [*nifāq*] and misguidance [*ḍalāl*] as the worst maladies of human society. These spiritual maladies subject society to a variety of problems and adversity, and their cure can be found in the Qur'an: "It contains a cure for the biggest diseases, namely unbelief, hypocrisy, revolt and misguidance."

Imām 'Alī (*'a*) does not mean that the Qur'an, like a medical prescription, explains physical ailments and prescribes a medicine for every sickness, or provides solutions for all economic and military problems, and formulas that can be used in the fields of technology and industry. Anyone who has the least knowledge of life in this world knows that problems require their respective natural means and ways. As stated before, in solving these problems the Holy Qur'an states the general ways which can be understood and followed by using our God-given intellect, talents and the acquired knowledge in human sciences.

At this point, let me draw the attention of the dear readers to two points:

The first is that natural causes and physical factors have their own effects and outcomes but it is necessary to note that the First Cause of all phenomena is God, the Blessed and Exalted. It is He who has created the system of the universe, based it upon the cause and effect relationship, and it is He who grants causality to the causes and factors. Without His ontological will, no agent can have independence in the effect of his action. Therefore, in curing all ailments and solving all problems and difficulties, we must essentially turn to God, the Exalted, and pin our hopes on Him. It is true that in solving problems and curing ailments, we resort to natural sources but as demanded by monotheism the cure and solution to problems must essentially be expected and regarded as coming from Him.

The second point is that the way of solving problems and curing ailments should not be considered as solely depending on natural causes and physical solutions. It is incorrect to think that in the absence of natural causes and physical factors or their inefficiency in solving problems, it is impossible to solve a problem, recover from a sickness, cure ailments, or fulfill any legitimate and rightful demand of man. By creating the system of cause and effect, God, the Exalted, has not made Himself unable to create phenomenon through an unnatural way. Rather, the precedent of Allah is that initially affairs are conducted through natural agents but are not confined only to natural agents. In fact, quite often, God created things through unnatural means and this can also be called divine precedent. Curing or treating a disease can possibly be done through natural ways and medical treatment, or under special circumstances, through unnatural means such as the supplications of the infallible Imāms (*'a*) or other *awliyā'* [saints] of Allah. In the same manner, the combatants of monotheism, who from the perspective of material equipment were condemned to be defeated by the enemy on the battlefield, emerged victorious owing to hidden help and unnatural causes. Such instances can be regarded as part of the Divine causes and factors.

The Holy Qur'an has narrated events that came to pass through unnatural ways. For example, for rain to fall according to its natural course and factors, the water of the seas and oceans must evaporate and turn into clouds. Then, because of the difference between sea and land temperatures, the wind tends to scatter the clouds to other parts of the earth until the drops of water in the clouds fall in the form of raindrops, snow drops or hailstones. To expect rain without its natural causes and factors according to the scientific perspective is regarded as irrational and futile. However, without considering the natural factors of rain, Ḥaḍrat Nūḥ (Noah) (*'a*) addressed his community [*qawm*] and urged them to repent and ask for forgiveness so that the sky would send down rain:

﴿ وَيَا قَوْمِ اسْتَغْفِرُوا رَبَّكُمْ ثُمَّ تُوبُوا إِلَيْهِ يُرْسِلِ السَّمَاءَ عَلَيْكُم مِّدْرَارًا وَيَزِدْكُمْ قُوَّةً إِلَى قُوَّتِكُمْ وَلَا تَتَوَلَّوْا مُجْرِمِينَ ﴾

> *"O my people! Plead with your Lord for forgiveness, then turn to Him penitently: He will send copious rains for you from the sky, and add power to your [present] power. So do not turn your backs [on Him] as guilty ones."*[1]

It is true that the natural causes and factors of rain and the entire system of cause and effect governing the nature are all under divine power and the will of God, but without taking them into account God, the Exalted, says to

1 *Sūrah Hūd* 11:52.

the people: "Ask forgiveness for your sins and turn to God. In turn, He will send copious rains from the sky."

One may possibly say that God, the Exalted, does not mean that without the presence of natural causes, there will be no rain; rather, it means that He will send down rain for us by means of facilitating natural causes. The reply is that this notion is inconsistent with the monotheistic viewpoint because as stated earlier, by creating the system of cause and effect, God, the Exalted, has not made Himself unable to create phenomena without natural causes and factors. Regarding His power in creating and bringing phenomena into being, God says:

﴿ إِنَّمَا أَمْرُهُ إِذَا أَرَادَ شَيْئًا أَنْ يَقُولَ لَهُ كُنْ فَيَكُونُ ﴾

"When He wills something, all He needs to do is to say to it, 'Be,' and it is."[1]

The wisdom behind some calamities

In addition to the above subject, sometimes the wisdom of God, the Exalted, demands that He showers His blessings upon His servants through unnatural ways. In doing so, He creates factors different from the known physical ones for people who deserve His mercy. The system of creation is anchored in wisdom, and the purpose of creating man is guidance and perfection. Guidance and perfection can be achieved through gnosis, reflection on the divine verses, servitude, and acting upon the commandments of the divine prophets (*'a*) and the religion of truth. Yet, sometimes, people stray from the path of truth on account of sin and wrongdoing. Usually, when human beings are materially well off and economically well heeled, they pay less attention to God and spirituality. At that time, their human and divine qualities become weak and finally disappear. As a result, the ground for insolence, disbelief, deviation, and misguidance opens up for them.

The Qur'an states:

﴿ كَلَّا إِنَّ الْإِنسَانَ لَيَطْغَى * أَن رَّآهُ اسْتَغْنَى ﴾

"Indeed man becomes rebellious when he considers himself without need."[2]

If the dominant spirit of the majority in a society is that of arrogance and insolence, divine grace and favor demand that He warn the people in one

---

1 *Sūrah Yā-Sīn* 36:82.

2 *Sūrah al-'Alaq* 96:6-7.

... awaken them from the slumber of heedlessness and ... the path of truth and servitude. In order to realize this, ... cts them with calamities in the forms of poverty and ... usly, He introduces repentance, asking for forgiveness of ... to Him through prayer and supplication to remove those ca... finally the purpose of creation, which is nothing but the voluntary desire for perfection in man, can be realized. This process is also one of the astounding precedents of God. He sometimes sent a prophet and subjected his community to hardships so that they would not become heedless of Him and the path of truth, and be protected from the devastation of material pleasures.

Under difficult conditions human beings realize their spiritual needs and are more inclined to accept the truth and the teachings of the prophets (*'a*), compared to the time when they are in comfort. The Qur'an states:

﴿ وَمَا أَرْسَلْنَا فِي قَرْيَةٍ مِّن نَّبِيٍّ إِلاَّ أَخَذْنَا أَهْلَهَا بِالْبَأْسَاء وَالضَّرَّاء لَعَلَّهُمْ يَضَّرَّعُونَ ﴾

> *"We did not send a prophet to any town without visiting its people with stress and distress so that they might entreat [for Allah's forgiveness]."*[1]

Verses 75 and 76 of *Sūrah al-Mu'minūn* also explain this subject:

﴿ وَلَوْ رَحِمْنَاهُمْ وَكَشَفْنَا مَا بِهِم مِّن ضُرٍّ لَّلَجُّوا فِي طُغْيَانِهِمْ يَعْمَهُونَ * وَلَقَدْ أَخَذْنَاهُم بِالْعَذَابِ فَمَا اسْتَكَانُوا لِرَبِّهِمْ وَمَا يَتَضَرَّعُونَ ﴾

> *"Should We have mercy upon them and remove their distress from them, they would surely persist, bewildered in their rebellion. Certainly We have seized them with punishment, yet they neither humbled themselves before their Lord, nor did they entreat [Him for mercy]."*[2]

Therefore, the philosophy behind some afflictions and difficulties is to awaken people and make them return to the path of guidance, although it is possible that these calamities do not awaken some communities as they remain stubborn in their deviation and misguidance. In this case, the guidance [*ḥujjah*] is exhausted for them and they have to accept responsibility for the sure calamity that will put an end to their lives.

In verses 42 to 44 of *Sūrah al-An'ām*, the Qur'an addresses the Prophet of Islam (*ṣ*) thus:

---

1 *Sūrah al-A'rāf* 7:94.

2 *Sūrah al-Mu'minūn* 23:75-76.

﴿ وَلَقَدْ أَرْسَلنَا إِلَى أُمَمٍ مِّن قَبْلِكَ فَأَخَذْنَاهُمْ بِالْبَأْسَاء وَالضَّرَّاء لَعَلَّهُمْ يَتَضَرَّعُونَ * فَلَوْلا إِذْ جَاءهُمْ بَأْسُنَا تَضَرَّعُواْ وَلَـكِن قَسَتْ قُلُوبُهُمْ وَزَيَّنَ لَهُمُ الشَّيْطَانُ مَا كَانُواْ يَعْمَلُونَ * فَلَمَّا نَسُواْ مَا ذُكِّرُواْ بِهِ فَتَحْنَا عَلَيْهِمْ أَبْوَابَ كُلِّ شَيْءٍ حَتَّى إِذَا فَرِحُواْ بِمَا أُوتُواْ أَخَذْنَاهُم بَغْتَةً فَإِذَا هُم مُّبْلِسُونَ ﴾

"We have certainly sent [apostles] to nations before you, then We seized them with stress and distress so that they might entreat [Us]. Why did they not entreat when Our punishment overtook them! But their hearts had hardened, and Satan had made to seem decorous to them what they had been doing. So when they forgot what they had been admonished of, We opened for them the gates of all [good] things. When they rejoiced in what they were given, We seized them suddenly, whereat, behold, they were despondent."[1]

We have to know that this has been the precedent of God [*sunnat Allāh*] with respect to past communities and the *ummah* of the Last Apostle (*ṣ*) is not an exception to it.

For the people of insight and caution, calamities, problems and adversities act as reminders of guidance. As stated by the Qur'an, there are also people in their midst who are heedless and will not be awakened by any warning, alarm or reminder and come to their senses.

It is important to pay attention to the philosophy behind such events, learn a lesson from the past, repent and return to God. It is indeed a pity that in our society only a few pay attention to this matter. Owing to this heedlessness or weakness of faith, some officials extend their hands to other than God in a bid to be relieved from economic difficulties such as drought and famine. By allocating a huge budget from the public treasury, they intend to create rain by putting chemical elements in the clouds. How futile! Is the knowledge of the cause of rain by the emergence of clouds and their scattering by means of wind and other limited factors that makes man arrogant, thinking he can produce rain whenever he wants, and instead of drawing the attention of the Muslim masses to God and resorting to His favor and beneficence, he searches and hunts for a fragment of the clouds while on top of a mountain in order to impregnate it, so to speak, and thus send down rain?! By the way, the said issue calls to mind the story of Ḥaḍrat Nūḥ (*'a*) and his son. After 950 years of inviting them to faith, Ḥaḍrat Nūḥ (*'a*) was disappointed as his people refused to believe in God. After losing all hope of guiding them, and witnessing signs of divine wrath,

1 *Sūrah al-An'ām* 6:42-44.

he urged his son to believe in God and embark on the ark in order to be saved from the definite punishment. In reply to his father, he expressed his atheistic thought, thus:

﴿ سَآوِي إِلَى جَبَلٍ يَعْصِمُنِي مِنَ الْمَاء ﴾

> *"I shall take refuge on a mountain; it will protect me from the flood."*[1]

As we all know, he did not believe in God till the last moment and perished. By relating this story, God, the Exalted, reveals the essence of atheistic thought and warns people of it.

Now, this atheistic thought also exists among some people, especially the xenomaniac intellectuals. Instead of having faith in God and drawing the people toward Him in their speeches and writings, they expect and rely on the assistance of the enemies of Islam in solving problems.

It is known to those who are informed that we do not intend to oppose scientific advancement and the achievement of human sciences, because the Qur'an and monotheistic thought—more than any other school of thought—calls upon the people to learn and seek knowledge and make use of the products of human thought and ideas. At this juncture, what we emphatically oppose is this atheistic thought. Unfortunately, those who follow this school of thought are not few in our society.

In any case, the best, shortest and safest way of solving individual and social problems is to return to the Door of the House of God, for treading the way of God ensures our eternal and otherworldly salvation as well as removes our problems and hardships.

﴿ فَقُلْتُ اسْتَغْفِرُوا رَبَّكُمْ إِنَّهُ كَانَ غَفَّارًا * يُرْسِلِ السَّمَاء عَلَيْكُم مِّدْرَارًا ﴾

> *"Then I told [them]: 'Plead to your Lord for forgiveness. Indeed He is the All-forgiving. He will send for you abundant rains from the sky.'"*[2]

Therefore, in order to remove deficiencies and find relief from problems the Qur'an proposes solutions to its followers and guarantees the efficacy of these solutions. As experienced many times, the Muslims can try them.

Undoubtedly, the victory of the Islamic Revolution in Iran is one of the miraculous examples of the divine succor and hidden help of God to our

---

1 *Sūrah Hūd* 11:43.

2 *Sūrah Nūḥ* 71:10-11.

Islamic society. When all the people, by relying upon God and refusing to pin their hopes on other than Him, demanded an Islamic government, God—in accordance with His promise in the Qur'an: "O you who have faith! If you help Allah, He will help you and make your feet steady"[1]—made the people victorious over their enemies, notwithstanding the power of the 2,500-year-old monarchial regime backed up by all the enemies of Islam. The precedent of God, that when people turn to Him He shall help them, is still true. Once they forget God, seek assistance from other than Him, and turn their backs to Him, they shall incur wrath and ignominy.

Anyway, there is no doubt that the Holy Qur'an is the healing prescription of God, and the salvation of man in this world and the hereafter lies in abiding with its revitalizing injunctions. The way of solving individual and social problems must be sought in it. The Qur'an—this guarantor of the salvation of man—must be recognized and one must strive to respect and honor it and act upon its orders. However, there are two kinds of respect paid to the Qur'an, which we shall cite below.

Outward and real respect for the Holy Qur'an

The respect shown to the Qur'an today in Muslim societies can be called outward respect. The Holy Qur'an has not been revealed to us only to be treated with respect in manner and style. The Qur'an is not meant only for memorization and recitation in a melodious voice. The Qur'an is the book of life and its divine messages must be followed in his life so as to attain salvation in this world and the hereafter. Government officials in Muslim countries are particularly obliged to organize and implement the overall political policies in accordance with the instructions of this divine book so as to pave the ground for the growth of a Qur'anic culture among the members of society and thus realize the purpose behind the revelation of the Qur'an, which is nothing but the perfection and felicity of man under the blessing of justice and equity on earth.

Unfortunately, the necessity of taking the Qur'an as the axis of the sociopolitical lives of Muslims has been neglected. Now, institutions, from preschool to the tertiary level in many Muslim countries, are engaged in teaching and learning the Holy Qur'an, busy teaching the reading, recitation and memorization of the Qur'an through various methods. Every year, we witness international competitions on the memorization and recitation of the Holy Qur'an. Various sciences of the Qur'an such as *tajwīd*, *tartīl* and others occupy a special place among those who are fond of the Qur'an. In addition, the Qur'an is held in high esteem among Muslim masses, such that

1 *Sūrah Muḥammad* 47:7.

they do not touch its words and verses without ablution, and sit humbly while reading it. Many of them do not stretch their feet against a copy of the Qur'an. They cover it with the best of covers and place it in attractive boxes. In sum, such outward forms of respect to the Qur'an are common among Muslim masses.

The observance of the abovementioned forms of respect to this heavenly book is a necessary value. No matter how faithful we are to such practices, we have not paid due respect to this heavenly book and have not expressed due gratitude for this greatest blessing of God, the Exalted, which is the blessing of guidance. However, the highest form of respect and gratitude for any blessing is to realize its essence and act upon it the way God has commanded. Once we consider the Qur'an with this perspective and pay respect and honor to it, it will become clear that the Holy Qur'an does not have a desirable place in the culture of Muslim societies and due respect and honor are not being paid to it. The forms of paying respect to the Holy Qur'an by Muslims are necessary but by doing so, the purpose of God Almighty in revealing the Qur'an is not realized. Familiarity with the outward aspects of the Qur'an, reading its divine verses and paying outward respect to this curing prescription are a prelude to acting upon its instructions and injunctions. The true right of the Qur'an cannot be given without making it the axis of the sociopolitical lives of the Muslims.

Evidently, kissing and paying respect to a doctor's medical prescription and reading it in a melodious tone without understanding and abiding with its recommendations and instructions can never cure the disease of a patient. Every rational person believes that recovery lies in following the instructions of a medical prescription. The real form of respect to a medical prescription is to act upon it and not to offer outward respect to the doctor and his prescription.

The Qur'an as the true light

One of the demonstrative manifestations of God is light. God has likened Himself to light, saying: ﴿ اللَّهُ نُورُ السَّمَاوَاتِ وَالْأَرْضِ ﴾ *"Allah is the Light of the heavens and the earth."*[1] It is because of this light of God, the Exalted, that the world of being exists, and the blessing of existence continuously descends upon the creatures from its Source. As such, the phenomena and creatures subsist.

Sometimes, the word of God is also described as "light", for it is by means of light that man finds his way and is saved from wandering and getting

1 *Sūrah al-Nūr* 24:35.

lost. Since the most disastrous misguidance in the path (
endangers the salvation of man, the real and true light
human beings from misguidance and clearly shows the
perfection. In other words, it distinguishes the patl
salvation from the paths of degradation and deviation. As such,
Exalted, has described the Qur'an as "light", saying:

﴿ قَدْ جَاءَكُم مِّنَ اللَّهِ نُورٌ وَكِتَابٌ مُّبِينٌ ﴾

> *"Certainly there has come to you a light from Allah and a manifest Book"*[1]

As such, by benefiting from it, you can distinguish the path of felicity from that of perdition.

After describing Islam and the Apostle (*ṣ*), Ḥaḍrat 'Alī (*'a*) thus says in Sermon 189 while describing the Holy Qur'an:

ثُمَّ أَنْزَلَ عَلَيْهِ الْكِتَابَ نُوراً لاَ تُطْفَأُ مَصَابِيحُهُ، وَسِرَاجاً لاَ يَخْبُو تَوَقُّدُهُ، وَبَحْراً لاَ يُدْرَكُ قَعْرُهُ.

> "Then, Allah sent to him the Book as a 'light' whose flames cannot be extinguished, a 'lamp' whose gleam does not die, and a 'sea' whose depth cannot be sounded."[2]

In describing the Qur'an in this sermon by using three extremely beautiful similes, Ḥaḍrat 'Alī (*'a*) wants to acquaint the hearts of the Muslims with the greatness of the Qur'an and draw their attention towards this magnificent divine asset which has been at their disposal.

Initially, Imām 'Alī (*'a*) describes the Qur'an as a "light" whose flames cannot be extinguished and whose gleam does not die. Through a similitude of what is intelligible to what is perceptible, he says that the Qur'an is like the great source of electric energy that illuminates the highways that are running in different directions in the darkness of the night through a network of powerful electric lights. By installing traffic lights along crossroads, it distinguishes the way that leads to a specific destination from those other ways that end up in terrible abysses for those who want to arrive safely at their destination. The Qur'an also plays the same role in a religious or Islamic society with a difference: the flames emanating from this source of light and illuminating the path of salvation can never be extinguished. As such, the path of truth is always straight and illuminated, and the Holy

---

1 *Sūrah al-Mā'idah* 5:15.

2 *Nahj al-Balāghah*, Sermon 189.

Qur'an and the glowing flames emanating from it continuously warn its followers to be careful and not deviate from the path of truth.

In another part of the sermon, Imām 'Alī (*'a*) says:

وَنُوراً لَيْسَ مَعَهُ ظُلْمَةٌ.

"[The Qur'an is] an effulgence with which there is no darkness."[1]

This is because this heavenly book has innate beacons which incessantly illuminate the path of guidance and felicity. The Imāms (*'a*) who are the interpreters of divine revelation represent the beacons that impart the knowledge of the Qur'an to the people and acquaint them with its truth through their God-endowed knowledge.

Qur'anic lamps and reflections

As we know, according to the Tradition on Two Weighty Things [*ḥadīth al-thaqalayn*], the Qur'an and the *'itrat* [progeny of the Prophet (ṣ)]—these two divine assets along the path of guidance of the monotheists—are complementary. By clinging to one and abandoning the other, the purpose behind the revelation of the Qur'an cannot be realized. The infallible Imāms (*'a*) are lamps whose lights emanate from this divine source and possess the sciences of the Qur'an and its truth. These holy personages can distinguish the metaphorical [*mutashābihāt*] from the precise verses [*muḥkamāt*] and the true path from the false one, and guide people toward the path of salvation and perfection. Meanwhile, the people are supposed to learn the sciences of the Qur'an from them and act upon them.

God's precedent [*sunnat Allāh*] is such that the people have to be acquainted with the sciences of the Qur'an through the *Ahl al-Bayt* (*'a*) and strive to ensure their own salvation in this world and the hereafter by abiding by them. Hence, by instituting the unbroken chain of Imamate [*imāmah*], God, the Exalted, has kept open the way of benefiting from the sciences of the Qur'an for those who are in search of salvation. The enemies and materialists throughout history have tried to extinguish the light of divine guidance which is embodied in the school of the *Ahl al-Bayt* (*'a*) but the Qur'an states that they will never succeed in doing so:

﴿ يُرِيدُونَ لِيُطْفِؤُوا نُورَ اللَّهِ بِأَفْوَاهِهِمْ وَاللَّهُ مُتِمُّ نُورِهِ وَلَوْ كَرِهَ الْكَافِرُونَ ﴾

"They desire to put out the light of Allah with their mouths, but Allah shall perfect His light though the faithless should be averse."[1]

---

1 *Ibid.*

As such, Ḥaḍrat ‘Alī (*‘a*) likens the Qur’an with a lamp whose flames cannot be extinguished and whose gleam does not die.

The sciences of the Qur’an are so profound and extensive that whenever those who are familiar with the knowledge of the *Ahl al-Bayt* (*‘a*) contemplate on them, they acquire new knowledge and facts at every stage. As this heavenly book is a manuscript of divine knowledge, however much those who are thirsty of the truth drink from its pure fountain their thirst is never quenched. In fact, they become thirstier. As such, we can see that by reciting divine verses in ritual prayers and reflecting upon them, the *awliyā’* of Allah and those who are knowledgeable of the truth of the Qur’an strive to purify their souls and place themselves more than ever at the threshold of the inspirations of God and His infinite knowledge. The Qur’an is a radiant sun whose gnosis [*ma‘rifah*] is endless and whose luminosity is eternal, for this heavenly book is like a deep ocean. It is impossible for anyone to fathom it expect the Apostle (*ṣ*) and the infallible Imāms (*‘a*) who possess the “knowledge of the Book” [*‘ilm al-kitāb*]. Any person who wants to be familiar with the Qur’an or the Word of God and lead his individual or social life based upon the instructions of this heavenly book has no option but to cling to the Qur’an according to the interpretation, explanation and conduct of the Apostle (*ṣ*) and the infallible Imāms (*‘a*). In proving this, we shall point to certain parts of two traditions:

Imām al-Ṣādiq (*‘a*) says:

وَنَحْنُ قَنَادِيْلُ النُّبُوَّةِ وَمَصَابِيْحُ الرِّسَالَةِ وَنَحْنُ نُوْرُ الأَنْوَارِ وَكَلِمَةُ الْجَبَّارِ وَنَحْنُ رَايَةُ الْحَقِّ الَّتِي مَنْ تَبِعَهَا نَجىٰ وَمَنْ تَأَخَّرَ عَنْهَا هَوىٰ وَنَحْنُ مَصَابِيْحُ الْمِشْكَاةِ الَّتِي فِيْهَا نُورُ النُّوْرِ.

“We are the lanterns of apostleship [*nubuwwah*] and the lamps of messengership [*risālah*]. We are the lights of the Light and the word of thc Almighty. We are the banner of truth; whoever follows it is saved and whoever abandons it goes astray. We are the lamps of the niche which contains the Light of lights.”[2]

A similar statement has also been reported from Imām al-Sajjād (*‘a*) when he said:

إِنَّ مَثَلَنَا فِي كِتَابِ اللهِ كَمَثَلِ الْمِشْكَاة وَالْمِشْكَاةُ فِي الْقَنْدِيْلِ فَنَحْنُ الْمِشْكَاةُ فِيْهَا مِصْبَاحٌ وَالْمِصْبَاحُ مُحَمَّدٌ (ص) أَلْمِصْبَاحُ فِي زُجَاجَةٍ نَحْنُ الزُّجَاجَةُ كَأَنَّهَا كَوْكَبٌ دُرِّيٌّ يُوقَدُ مِن شَجَرَةٍ مُبَارَكَةٍ زَيْتُونَةٍ مَعْرُوْفَةٍ لا شَرْقِيَّةٍ وَلا غَرْبِيَّةٍ لاَ مُنْكَرَةٍ وَلاَ دَعْيَةٍ يَكَادُ زَيْتُهَا يُضِيءُ وَلَوْ لَمْ

---

1 *Sūrah al-Ṣaff* 61:8.

2 *Biḥār al-Anwār*, vol. 26, p. 259.

تَمْسَسْهُ نَارٌ نُورٌ الْقُرْآنِ عَلَى نُورٍ يَهْدِي اللَّهُ لِنُورِهِ مَن يَشَاء وَيَضْرِبُ اللَّهُ الْأَمْثَالَ لِلنَّاسِ وَاللَّـهُ بِكُلِّ شَيْءٍ عَلِيمٌ بِأَنْ يَهْدِي مَنْ أَحَبَّ إِلىٰ وِلاَيَتِنَا.

> "Verily, our example in the Book of Allah is like the niche. We are the niche wherein a lamp is placed and the lamp is in a glass and the glass is Muḥammad (ṣ). (And) the glass is as it were a brightly shining star—lit from a blessed olive tree, neither eastern nor western, whose oil lights up, though fire does not touch it. The light of the Qur'an is light upon light. Allah guides to His Light whomever He wishes. Allah draws parables for mankind, and Allah has knowledge of all things. Verily, He guides whoever He loves to our guardianship [*wilāyah*]."[1]

In this saying, the Imām (*'a*) has interpreted verse 35 of *Sūrah al-Nūr* as referring to the Apostle (*ṣ*) and his *Ahl al-Bayt* (*'a*) or the infallible Imāms (*'a*). The Imām (*'a*) said that the similitude of the *Ahl al-Bayt* (*'a*) in the Qur'an is that of a transparent glass that reflects the light of the lamp of apostleship [*nubuwwah*]. This light emanates from a blessed tree whose radiance is all-encompassing and undeniable, overflowing with Divinc light. This light is neither eastern nor western and neither unknown nor manifest.

Imām al-Sajjād (*'a*) says that the truth of the Apostle (*ṣ*) and his holy *Ahl al-Bayt* (*'a*) is like a luminous lamp which gives light without a flame. The light of the Qur'an is the light (the *wilāyah* of the *Ahl al-Bayt* (*'a*)) by which God guides whomever He wishes.

Deliverance of the followers of the Qur'an on the Day of Resurrection

As pointed earlier, salvation is of paramount import for man, and life in this world is a prelude for eternal life in the next world. The similitude of man in this world in relation to the other world is that of a traveler who, by working hard day and night in a foreign city, living frugally, and sending his earnings to his motherland or birthplace, intends to build a house and have enough capital so that upon his return home, he can live comfortably with honor and dignity for the remaining part of his life—the only difference being that the otherworldly life is eternal and everlasting.

Man's beliefs and actions are seeds planted by him in this world which will yield fruit in the next world. If, in this world, a farmer plants a seed according to the instructions of an expert on agriculture, his yield at harvest time will be the best possible, quantitatively and qualitatively. Similarly, if human beings organize their actions and activities according to the

1 *Ibid.*, vol. 23, p. 314.

instructions of the Holy Qur'an and the teachings and precepts of the *Ahl al-Bayt* (*'a*) and set their individual and sociopolitical affairs according to the dictates of the Holy Qur'an, in addition to honor and glory in this world, they will enjoy the outcome of their good deeds in the hereafter.

Ḥaḍrat 'Alī (*'a*) calls upon people to preserve the enlivening ordinances of the Qur'an:

فَاسْأَلُوا اللهَ بِهِ، وَتَوَجَّهُوا إِلَيْهِ بِحُبِّهِ، وَلاَ تَسْأَلُوا بِهِ خَلْقَهُ، إِنَّهُ مَا تَوَجَّهَ الْعِبَادُ إِلَـى اللهِ بِمِثْلِـهِ وَاعْلَمُوا أَنَّهُ شَافِعٌ مُشَفَّعٌ، وَقَائِلٌ مُصَدَّقٌ، وَأَنَّهُ مَنْ شَفَعَ لَهُ الْقُرْآنُ يَوْمَ الْقِيَامَةِ شُفِّعَ فِيهِ، وَمَـنْ مَحَلَ بِهِ الْقُرْآنُ يَوْمَ الْقِيَامَةِ صُدِّقَ عَلَيْهِ

"Pray to Allah through it and turn to Allah with its love. Do not ask the people through it. There is nothing like it through which the people should turn to Allah, the Sublime. Know that it is an interceder and its intercession will be accepted. It is a trusted speaker. Whoever the Qur'an intercedes for on the Day of Judgment, its intercession will be accepted. He about whom the Qur'an speaks ill on the Day of Judgment shall testify to its truthfulness."[1]

After saying that the Qur'an is the greatest cure and solution to the ills of society, Imām 'Alī (*'a*) persuades people to look for the cure to their ills in the Qur'an by following it and turn to God by acting upon it, and not take the Qur'an as a means of asking other human beings for their help.

Then, the Imām (*'a*) warns the people of the danger of being separated from the Qur'an and invites them to follow this heavenly book and take it as the guideline in their thought and action:

فَإِنَّهُ يُنَادِي مُنَادٍ يَوْمَ الْقِيَامَةِ أَلاَ إِنَّ كُلَّ حَارِثٍ مُبْتَلىً فِي حَرْثِهِ وَعَاقِبَةِ عَمَلِـهِ، غَيْـرَ حَرَثَـةِ الْقُرْآنِ، فَكُونُوا مِنْ حَرَثَتِهِ وَأَتْبَاعِهِ، وَاسْتَدِلُّوهُ عَلى رَبِّكُمْ، وَاسْتَنْصِحُوهُ عَلى أَنْفُسِكُمْ، وَاتَّهِمُوا عَلَيْهِ آرَاءَكُمْ، وَاسْتَغِشُّوا فِيهِ أَهْوَاءَكُمْ

"On the Day of Judgment an announcer will announce, "Beware, every sower of a crop is in distress except the sowers of the Qur'an." Therefore, you should be among the sowers of the Qur'an and its followers. Make it guide you towards your Lord. Seek its

1 *Nahj al-Balāghah*, Sermon 175.

> advice for yourselves; do not trust your views against it; and regard your desires in the matter of the Qur'an as misguiding."[1]

On the Day of Resurrection, when human beings will be resurrected for their reckoning—recompense and punishment—an announcer will announce this truth to the people: "O people! Know that all human beings today will be afflicted with the products and outcome of what they sowed except those whose beliefs and actions are based upon injunctions and instructions of the Qur'an. Only these individuals will be pleased with the products and effects of their deeds and beliefs and not feel cheated.

Admonition and reminder

The life of all creatures including man is limited. This life begins at a certain point in time and ends with death at another point. During this limited span of time, man is always in a state of becoming and his personality in a state of formation. The personality of man results from his beliefs and convictions, actions and behavior. The actions of man will also be manifested on the Day of Resurrection and every person will be made to weep on viewing the product of his deeds.

The point to be highlighted here is that as long as man has not yet departed from this world, he can mend his past ways at any moment by assessing his thoughts, beliefs and actions and change his destiny toward deliverance and salvation in this world and the hereafter. Sometimes people come to their senses in a transforming moment and through real repentance and serious decision, they transform their gloomy past into a bright and prosperous future and traverse overnight a distance of a century's journey. It must be noted that the opportunity for assessment and mending is only possible in this world, for there will be no room for reform after death.

If man bases his deeds and activities on the Qur'an and the divine precepts and injunctions in this world, in the words of Ḥaḍrat 'Alī (*'a*), he will be among the sowers of the Qur'an, and, in the hereafter, enjoy the products of his deeds. The time for action and preparation exists only in this world:

أَلْيَوْمَ عَمَلٌ وَلاَ حِسَابَ وَغَدًا حِسَابٌ وَلاَ عَمَلَ.

> "Today is the time for action and not for reckoning while tomorrow is the time for reckoning and not for action."[2]

1 *Ibid.*

2 *Biḥar al-Anwār*, vol. 32, p. 354; vol. 77, p. 419.

Imām ‘Alī (*‘a*) who knows the reality of this world and the hereafter as well as their relation to each other and is highly concerned about the plight of the Muslims said: “You should be among the sowers of the Qur’an.” That is to say, “If you want salvation, you have to sow good deeds with the blessings of the Qur’an. Be among those who build their abodes in this world and the hereafter by acting upon the enlivening instructions of this heavenly book. Take the Qur’an as your guide so that you will never be in loss.”

The secret of success and the role of the Qur’an

It seems that in order to be successful in any program, especially in educational, cultural and social affairs, there are some basic conditions:

1. The correctness and accuracy of the program with respect to its goal;

2. Conviction and faith in the program and its procedures; and

3. Implementation of the instructions and procedures stated in the program.

Obviously, if any of the three conditions is not met, the efficiency of the program will suffer and the goal not achieved.

We all claim that the Qur’an is God’s word and a program of life for Muslims. Yet, mere claim or outward acknowledgment is not enough. Confession will be considered as faith in the Qur’an and its enlivening instructions, provided it demonstrates sincere belief and conviction and total submission to its divine message. Only then will the Qur’an become effective in guiding the society.

The Holy Qur’an says:

﴿ ذَلِكَ الْكِتَابُ لاَ رَيْبَ فِيهِ هُدًى لِّلْمُتَّقِينَ * الَّذِينَ يُؤْمِنُونَ بِالْغَيْبِ وَيُقِيمُونَ الصَّلاةَ وَمِمَّا رَزَقْنَاهُمْ يُنفِقُونَ * والَّذِينَ يُؤْمِنُونَ بِمَا أُنزِلَ إِلَيْكَ وَمَا أُنزِلَ مِن قَبْلِكَ وَبِالآخِرَةِ هُمْ يُوقِنُونَ * أُوْلَـئِكَ عَلَى هُدًى مِّن رَّبِّهِمْ وَأُوْلَـئِكَ هُمُ الْمُفْلِحُونَ ﴾

“This is the Book; there is no doubt in it, a guidance to the God-wary, who believe in the Unseen, and maintain the prayer, and spend out of what We have provided for them; and who believe in what has been sent down to you and what was sent down before you, and are certain of the Hereafter. Those who follow their Lord’s guidance, it is they who are the felicitous.”[1]

---

1 *Sūrah al-Baqarah* 2:2-5.

Of course, we are aware that faith [*īmān*] has various degrees, and the Islamic society can overcome its problems and achieve victory over the enemies with honor and dignity, provided that the cultural officials of society have sincere belief and faith in the religious government and submit to the precepts and decrees of the Qur'an like the submission of Prophet Ibrāhīm (Abraham) (*'a*), and do not feign belief in the Qur'an by using religion and religious culture only in order to gain popularity.

In the Holy Qur'an, those who do not have faith in the divine laws and ordinances and only pretend to have accepted Islam in order to deceive Muslims and attain their worldly objectives are described as *munāfiqīn* [hypocrites]. The external and internal characteristics and behavior of this group have been mentioned in numerous verses of the Holy Qur'an.

Ibrāhīm ('a) as a model of submission and servitude in the Holy Qur'an

The Holy Qur'an declares the submission of Ḥaḍrat Ibrāhīm (*'a*) to the divine commandments and orders, as the model of submission and resignation to the divine will, and presents faith, patience, fortitude, and reliance on God, the Exalted, as the secret of his success in facing problems and victory over the polytheists. It also urges us to have such faith and conviction vis-à-vis the command of God and the Holy Qur'an and to be as firm and resolute as Ibrāhīm (*'a*) in executing divine decrees.

Here, we shall briefly discuss the faith of Ḥaḍrat Ibrāhīm (*'a*) in executing God's command to sacrifice his son, Ḥaḍrat Ismā'īl (Ishmael) (*'a*), so that while explaining the spirit of God-centeredness in the monotheistic culture, we can point out our weakness in obeying the instructions of the Qur'an, and acquaint readers with the principal maladies of society.

It can be inferred from the Holy Qur'an that divine decree granted Ḥaḍrat Ibrāhīm (*'a*) a son after a hundred years. His wish came true after a very long period of expectation. Naturally, every person regards the existence of a righteous child as a continuation of his life. After the birth of Ismā'īl (*'a*), Ḥaḍrat Ibrāhīm (*'a*) was commanded by God, the Exalted, to take his child along with his magnanimous mother to the land of Mecca, leave them there in the most difficult conditions of the desert without trace of water and life, and return from Mecca after accomplishing his divine mission. After sometime, he was allowed to return to Mecca—when his son had grown up into a courteous and handsome youth whose rosy face removed the grief and sorrow of his father and made the pains of separation and problems easy for him. Unexpectedly, at the peak of emotional attachment to such a son, it was revealed to him in a "dream" that he had to sacrifice his son in the way of God. By the way, it is worthy to test our conviction and faith in God, the

Qur'an and the divine orders as well as the degrees of our submission to God by the faith and degree of submission of Ḥaḍrat Ibrāhīm (*'a*) so that we can discern the distance between us and what the Qur'an and God, the Exalted, want from us, and strengthen our faith. If you and I received an order from Jibra'īl (Archangel Gabriel) ('a) to sacrifice our own son—while we were awake and not in sleep—we cannot be sure of listening to it let alone executing the divine command to sacrifice our own son! Yet, without any hesitation, Ḥaḍrat Ibrāhīm (*'a*) was determined to obey the divine order. Without entertaining any doubt about the authenticity of what had been revealed to him he informed his son of his dream:

﴿ فَلَمَّا بَلَغَ مَعَهُ السَّعْيَ قَالَ يَا بُنَيَّ إِنِّي أَرَى فِي الْمَنَامِ أَنِّي أَذْبَحُكَ فَانظُرْ مَاذَا تَرَى قَالَ يَا أَبَتِ افْعَلْ مَا تُؤْمَرُ سَتَجِدُنِي إِن شَاءَ اللَّهُ مِنَ الصَّابِرِينَ ﴾

> *"When he was old enough to assist in his endeavor, he said, 'My son! I see in a dream that I am sacrificing you. Say what you think.' He said, 'Father! Do whatever you have been commanded to do. If Allah wishes, you will find me patient'."*[1]

Such is the degree of faith and submission of Ḥaḍrat Ibrāhīm (*'a*). Now, try to observe the degree of faith and submission of the son. Look at the obedience of the son to the command of God and his father, and you will be astonished by the sincerity and faith of individuals whom the pen and tongue are incapable of describing, and hesitate in calling yourselves "Muslims".

Ḥaḍrat Ismā'īl (*'a*)—this son who learned from his father the lesson of submission to the Will of God—encouraged his father to execute the divine order without asking about the philosophy behind killing him and induce doubt and hesitation in his father. He (*'a*) said: *"Father! Do whatever you have been commanded. If Allah wishes, you will find me patient."* Great men act after asking for the help of God, the Exalted, and rely on Him. In all activities, with His succor, assistance and utmost humbleness, they say: "By the will and help of God, I will perform such-and-such deed." Even here, Ḥaḍrat Ismā'īl (*'a*) did not rely on his own power but on Allah's help.

God, the Exalted, expresses and describes the visage of Ḥaḍrat Ibrāhīm (*'a*) and his state of submission to God by quoting Ibrāhīm's (*'a*) words:

﴿ إِنِّي وَجَّهْتُ وَجْهِيَ لِلَّذِي فَطَرَ السَّمَاوَاتِ وَالأَرْضَ حَنِيفًا وَمَا أَنَا مِنَ الْمُشْرِكِينَ ﴾

---

1 *Sūrah al-Ṣāffāt* 37:102.

> *"Indeed I have turned my face toward Him who originated the heavens and the earth, as a ḥanīf, and I am not one of the polytheists."*[1]

We must have the same belief and faith of Ibrāhīm (*'a*) in God and the Qur'an, to benefit from the Qur'an, i.e. guide society according to the instructions of the Qur'an.

Therefore, it is clear that in addition to faith and conviction, what will materialize the program on the guidance of the Qur'an is to act according to the instructions of the Qur'an and practice its enlivening commandments in both individual and social life. χ

1 *Sūrah al-An'ām* 6:79.

Chapter 2

Understanding and Interpreting the Qur'an

The main problem

In the previous chapter we arrived at the conclusion that the Qur'an is a book of divine guidance and all of us are duty-bound to believe it. We have to manage our lives and society according to its instructions so as to be felicitous in this world and the hereafter. Now I would like to pose this question: Notwithstanding the existence of the Qur'an, why do we still suffer from problems, especially cultural problems?

We will reply that it is because we do not act upon the salvation-giving commandments of the Qur'an as we ought to. This reply can be considered correct but it seems that the more fundamental question is: Why do we not act upon them as we ought to? In reality, what are the factors that contribute in the lesser attention given to the presence of the Qur'an in society and the gradual separation of people from the Qur'an, religious culture and divine values?

Since the subject of discussion is the Qur'an, according to *Nahj al-Balāghah*, we should ask: How does Ḥaḍrat 'Alī ('a) analyse the main problem of our society and what solution does he suggest? Before replying through a statement of Ḥaḍrat 'Alī ('a), I would like to embark on the main subject after a few preliminary remarks.

Faith in God and submission to the divine orders are among the most fundamental conditions of guidance and benefit from the instructions of the Holy Qur'an. Abrahamic faith and submission are necessary for one to be safe from the snares of Satan. The pebbles in Mash'ar al-Ma'rifah[1] must be collected with which to pelt [*ramy*] the devil of the commanding self or carnal soul [*nafs al-'ammārah*] when referring to the Holy Qur'an. One must resist one's carnal desires, give preference to the word of God over them, and have no preconceived notions, in order to avoid committing errors while referring to the divine verses and understanding the Holy Qur'an. It is not true that whoever approaches the Qur'an with whatever intentions and by whatever means can rightly benefit from it. Simply put it, if we have truly accepted the servitude to God, we have to totally submit to Him, resign to His will and decree and sincerely believe that He knows better than His servants what is good for them and that He bids or forbids whatever is good or bad for them. It is only with such faith and conviction that people can correctly understand this divine book and benefit from its enlivening instructions.

Therefore, the first and foremost condition of benefiting from the divine guidance is to have the spirit of submission and avoid any form of prejudgment and self-centeredness. In the prescription that he writes for a patient, an expert physician expects him to take the prescribed medicine and foods and prohibit the intake of medicine or foods that prevent or delay his recovery. Yet, are all prescriptions of a doctor consistent with the likes and inclinations of a patient? Possibly, a patient may enthusiastically take prescribed medicines and avoid some foods prohibited by the doctor. But in most cases, the inclinations of the patient are inconsistent with the prescriptions of the doctor. Sometimes, a patient wants to eat pickles but for the doctor, doing so is like taking deadly poison. In these cases, it is possible that because of his strong inclination to these foods, the patient would doubt the diagnosis of the doctor and make personal desire a justification for consuming them. Of course, regarding physical illnesses, on account of a strong desire to recover, man is not willing to violate the doctor's prescriptions. In most cases, he tries to prefer them over his personal inclinations and faithfully abide by the prescriptions of the attending physician. Concerning spiritual maladies, however, many people take their carnal inclinations as the criterion for judgment and engage in interpreting religion and divine laws on the basis of false, preconceived notions and improper desires.

---

1 Mash'ar al-Ma'rifah [lit. consciousness of the divine gnosis], Mash'ar al-Ḥarām [lit. sacred consciousness] or Muzdalifah: the place where the *Ḥajj* pilgrims spend the night on their return from 'Arafah to pick up 70 pebbles to be pelted [*ramy*] at *jamarāt* [places of the three stone slabs symbolizing Satan] in Mīnā. [Trans.]

Obviously, with such a mentality it is impossible to correctly understand the Qur'an and religion even if we assume that a person really wants to correctly understand it and has no intention at all to deceive others. The mere fact that he wants to understand the Qur'an and religion does not totally hinder the effects of his prejudgment, tainted notions and carnal inclinations from erroneously interpreting and understanding Qur'anic verses and traditions. Of course, the case of individuals who are aware and consciously distort religious laws and decrees to deceive the people and render a blow to the religious culture of society in the name of different interpretations is a different story which we will deal at its appropriate time. We will briefly examine the causes and motives of this anti-religious idea from the perspective of *Nahj al-Balāghah.* Now, we will try to find the proper way of referring to the Qur'an and understanding its laws and injunctions from the statements of Ḥaḍrat 'Alī (*'a*).

The advise of 'Alī ('a) in dealing with the Qur'an

After the luminous statement in which he gave the news of the Day of Resurrection, the pleasure of the followers of the Qur'an on their actions and past record and the affliction of the violators of the Qur'an on that day, Imām 'Alī (*'a*) advises the people, thus: "You should be among the institutors of the Qur'an and its followers. Make it your guide towards your Lord. Seek its advice for yourselves."[1] That is to say, "Know God through His Word. Know the attributes of the Lord through the Qur'an. The Qur'an is a guide that will lead you to God. You have to consult this divine guide so as to know its messenger and have faith in God who reveals the Qur'an. You human beings are in need of the One who is benevolent and compassionate to you so as to advise and sympathize with you in times of necessity. Take the Qur'an as your adviser and follow its sympathetic pieces of advice, for the Qur'an will never betray you but guide you in the best possible manner towards the straight path."

Ḥaḍrat 'Alī ('a) advises Muslims and those who are looking for felicity in this world and the hereafter to take the Qur'an as their guide and pay heed to its sincere admonitions, for

1 *Nahj al-Balāghah*, Sermon 175.

﴿إِنَّ هَـذَا الْقُرْآنَ يِهْدِي لِلَّتِي هِيَ أَقْوَمُ وَيُبَشِّرُ الْمُؤْمِنِينَ الَّذِينَ يَعْمَلُونَ الصَّالِحَاتِ أَنَّ لَهُمْ أَجْراً كَبِيراً﴾

"Indeed this Qur'an guides to what is most upright, and gives the good news to the faithful who do righteous deeds that there is a great reward for them."[1]

The point which is emphasized is the necessity for firm belief in the content of this noble verse, for once such faith in the Qur'an does not exist in man and he does not totally submit himself to God and empty himself of prejudgments and carnal desires, it is possible for him to succumb to satanic temptations and go astray. Once he consults the Qur'an, he unconsciously looks for verses that seemingly concord with his carnal desires.

Obviously, the injunctions and decrees of the Qur'an are not harmonious with the carnal desires and bestial inclinations of man. Thus, whenever the Qur'an states something against his personal inclinations, he is displeased and whenever Qur'anic verses are consistent with his carnal inclinations, he accepts them with open arms. Of course, all these reactions are expressed secretly in his heart but their effects are manifested through his actions and behavior. As such, reason demands that before consulting the Qur'an, man empties his mind of any form of self-centeredness so that he can enter the school of the Qur'an with a spirit of God-centeredness. It is in this manner, observing the etiquettes sincerely, that man acquires divine gnosis.

Speculative interpretation [tafsīr bi 'r-ra'y]

Obviously, to do the above is not an easy task. In fact, for those who do not have a strong spirit of servitude to God it is even more difficult. For this reason, it is called greater *jihād* [*jihād al-akbar*].

It seems that the psychological and mental ground of speculative interpretation [*tafsīr bi'r-ra'y*] is that man cannot abandon his carnal desires and inclinations. Satan further exploits this condition and directs the mind and thinking of such a person towards an erroneous and misleading interpretation of the Qur'an and religion. If the person has a good social standing, the temptation of Satan, the sworn enemy of mankind, is multiplied because he knows that by misguiding such a person, he would possibly misguide a group of people who listens to that person. We often find individuals issue religious edicts without consulting the Qur'an and, without the least required intellectual and academic merit and qualification, express their personal opinion and say that the Qur'an also affirms it. Then

---

1 *Sūrah al-Isrā'* (or *Banī Isrā'īl*) 17:9.

they justify it with short verses and their ambiguous outward meanings. Obviously, such a psychological background with preconceived notions does not guarantee an accurate understanding of the Qur'an but it also leads to misunderstanding and deviation from the truth.

In the religious parlance, this type of understanding and interpretation of the Qur'an is described as *"speculative interpretation"* [*tafsīr bi'r-ra'y*] and regarded as the worst kind of approach to the Qur'an, in particular, and religion, in general. The Qur'an considers this kind of approach to religion and divine verses as an act of mockery and categorically denounces it:

﴿ وَلاَ تَتَّخِذُوا آيَاتِ اللّهِ هُزُوًا وَاذْكُرُوا نِعْمَتَ اللّهِ عَلَيْكُمْ وَمَا أَنزَلَ عَلَيْكُمْ مِّنَ الْكِتَابِ وَالْحِكْمَةِ يَعِظُكُم بِهِ وَاتَّقُواْ اللّهَ وَاعْلَمُوا أَنَّ اللّهَ بِكُلِّ شَيْءٍ عَلِيمٌ ﴾

> *"Do not take the signs of Allah in derision, and remember Allah's blessings upon you, and what He has sent down to you of the Book and wisdom, to advise you therewith. Be wary of Allah, and know that Allah has knowledge of all things."*[1]

As mentioned earlier, the ones who benefit from the guidance of the Qur'an are those who believe and have faith in it. Those who want to coin religious or Qur'anic justification for their personal inclinations and interpret the Word of God according to their personal opinion have actually no faith in God. It is proper here to pay attention to some pertinent traditions:

قَالَ رَسُوْلُ اللهِ (ص): قَالَ اللهُ جَلَّ جَلاَلُهُ مَا آمَنَ بِي مَنْ فَسَّرَ بِرَأْيِهِ كَلاَمِي

The Messenger of Allah (ṣ) said:

> "Allah, may He be glorified, said: 'He who interprets My Word according to his opinion has indeed no faith in Me'."[2]

Meanwhile, the Apostle (ṣ) is also reported to have said:

مَنْ فَسَّرَ الْقُرْآنَ بِرَأْيِهِ فَقَدِ افْتَرىٰ عَلىٰ اللهِ الْكَذِبَ.

> "He who interprets the Qur'an according to his opinion has attributed a lie to Allah."[3]

Thus, one who intends to interpret Qur'anic verses in his favor and present it as the interpretation of the Qur'an or the Word of God, has actually set his opinion as the criterion, and attributes it to God, the Exalted. This approach

1 *Sūrah al-Baqarah* 2:231.

2 Shaykh al-Ṣadūq, *Al-Tawḥīd*, p. 68.

3 *Biḥār al-Anwār*, vol. 36, p. 227.

to the Qur'an and its interpretation is abominable and dangerous because it misguides, and those who commit such a sin shall be afflicted with the severest of punishments on the Day of Judgment. In this regard, the Apostle (ṣ) has also said:

مَنْ فَسَّرَ الْقُرْآنَ بِرَأْيِهِ فَلْيَتَبَوَّأْ مَقْعَدَهُ مِنَ النَّارِ.

> "The abode of the one who interprets the Qur'an according to his opinion shall be in the Fire."[1]

Therefore, in order to be safe from the gravest chastisement one should avoid impugning God, the Exalted, and keep away from falling into the pitfall of deviation, abandon carnal desires, shun egoism, have faith in the Sacred Essence, who is pure and good and does not wish anything but good for mankind, be God-oriented, and submit himself to Him.

The instruction of 'Alī ('a) to avoid speculative interpretation

As mentioned earlier, man has desires and notions which are sometimes, nay in most cases, inconsistent with the Qur'anic outlook. In accordance with his human nature, he also wants the Qur'an to affirm his views and desires. Sometimes, it is even possible that those notions unconsciously affect his understanding and interpretation of the Qur'an. Satan is busy looking for an opportunity to mislead a group of people from the path of truth by deceiving intellectuals who claim to be religious scholars. Hence, it is worthy to pay due attention to this part of the statement of Ḥaḍrat 'Alī (*'a*).

In a bid to be immune from erroneous understanding and avoid possible deviation, Imām 'Alī (*'a*) said:

وَاتَّهِمُوا عَلَيْهِ آرَاءَكُمْ.

> "Do not trust your views against it (the Qur'an)."[2]

That is to say, "When you engage in understanding and interpreting the Qur'an, find fault with your prejudgments, preconceived notions, inclinations, and views vis-à-vis the Qur'an and set aside your personal opinion and carnal desires." Imām 'Alī (*'a*) said,

> "Regard your desires in the matter of the Qur'an as deceitful."[3]

---

1 *'Awālī al-La'ālī,* vol. 4, p. 104.

2 *Nahj al-Balāghah,* Sermon 175.

3 *Ibid.*

It is said that the abovementioned statement indicates the need for utmost care, trustworthiness and God-wariness [*taqwā*] in understanding and interpreting the Holy Qur'an, for the Imām (*'a*) said that one should approach the Qur'an and embark on understanding and interpreting it with the assumption that he knows nothing and whatever it states is the truth:

وَاسْتَغِشُّوا فِيهِ أَهْوَاءَكُمْ.

"Regard your desires in the matter of the Qur'an as deceitful."[1]

That is to say, "Consider your desires as wrong and improper so that you can benefit much from the Qur'an. Otherwise, you will always be on the verge of error and deviation."

Therefore, the kernel of religion which is nothing but submission to God demands that man completely obeys God, the Exalted, and treats as erroneous his personal opinion with respect to God's decrees and injunctions in the Holy Qur'an. Once such a spirit dominates, it is obvious that he will grasp the divine ordinances, commandments and teachings of the Qur'an better, and once he totally surrenders to God, heartily accepts them.

Two perspectives on the Qur'an and religious teachings

There are two different perspectives on dealing with the Holy Qur'an and religious teachings:

1. Perspective based on God centeredness and the spirit of submission and servitude to Him, and

2. Perspective which regards the carnal desires of man as the essence of creation and tries to interpret and understand religious texts and teachings of the Qur'an on that basis—commonly known today as "humanism"; that is, man-centeredness vis-à-vis God-centeredness.

It seems that the abovementioned classification is beyond the previous subjects and discussions, for it is now assumed that there are two possible ways of understanding the Qur'an. One is anchored in the spirit of submission and servitude to God and the other is probably an effect of the carnal desires. Accordingly, in order to avoid speculative interpretation in understanding and interpreting the Qur'an and understand it accurately, we explained the pertinent advice of Ḥaḍrat 'Alī (*'a*) on the necessity of shunning prejudgment and purging the mind of carnal desires. In this perspective, we considered both groups of addressees of Imām 'Alī (*'a*) as

1 *Ibid.*

Muslims. In a bid to avoid deviation in religion and fall into the abyss of *tafsīr bi'r-ra'y*, the observance of piety and keeping aloof from carnal desire and prejudgment is indispensable. As we delve deeper into the issue, we find out the marvels of Imām 'Alī's ('a) words in classifying human beings on their degree of servitude to God into two main groups, and be more acquainted with his psychological knowledge of the human psyche in relation to religion and divine commandments.

By describing the characteristics of each group, he (*'a*) presents the two groups as follows:

1. One group consists of those who have completely acknowledged their servitude to God and are determined to combat their carnal desires and give precedence to the will and pleasure of God over their whims and caprice. Naturally, such individuals who heartily acknowledge this heavenly book, i.e. the Qur'an, sincerely accept its injunctions and teachings and take it as their guide in practice and strive to observe its rites.

In describing this group, Ḥaḍrat 'Alī (*'a*) said:

عِبَادَ اللهِ، إنَّ مِنْ أَحَبِّ عِبَادِ اللهِ إلَيْهِ عَبْداً أَعَانَهُ اللهُ عَلَى نَفْسِهِ.

> "Indeed, the most beloved of Allah is he whom Allah has given power (to act) against his passions."[1]

Then, Imām 'Alī (*'a*) stated the status of the Qur'an among these people:

قَدْ أَمْكَنَ الْكِتَابَ مِنْ زِمَامِهِ، فَهُوَ قَائِدُهُ وَإمَامُهُ، يَحُلُّ حَيْثُ حَلَّ ثَقَلُهُ، وَيَنْزِلُ حَيْثُ كَانَ مَنْزِلُهُ.

> "There is no good which he has not aimed at or any likely place (of virtue) of the Qur'an. Therefore the Qur'an is his guide and leader. He gets down when the Qur'an puts down his weight and he settles where the Qur'an settles him down."[2]

This group has accepted the Qur'an and the truths of religion as a set of objective realities and has faith in them. It regards religious ordinances and injunctions of the Holy Qur'an as containing objective realities and observes them as directly related to his salvation and their violation as the cause of perdition in this world and the hereafter.

Since these individuals have no opinion or view of their own, they believe in religion, heavenly scriptures, divine ordinances and teachings; have faith in the causative relationship between them and the welfare of mankind,

---

1 *Nahj al-Balāghah*, Sermon 86.

2 *Ibid.*

strive hard to accurately understand the Qur'an to know exactly what it enjoins; and then, follow it.

2. Opposed to the first group, there are people who think that the Qur'an, or any other religious text or scripture for that matter depends on what individuals think and it does not speak about absolute and specific subject matters. The Qur'an or any religious text is devoid of meaning and content and it has no innate purpose. Every person has his own ideas which stem from his educational, family, social and other backgrounds. Once he approaches the Qur'an, he deduces certain points based on his personal ideas, while the Qur'an does not actually express those points. In fact, it is his understanding which is discussed under the guise of the Qur'an. Obviously, given such perspective and outlook, religion, the Qur'an and its verses and injunctions are treated as words and frameworks devoid of any content and it is the ideas of man that give meaning and concept to these words. According to the abovementioned notion, it is claimed that the Qur'an or any religious text has nothing to speak of. Rather, every person understands something from the Qur'an or any religious text according to his own mindset. Obviously, this kind of outlook is actually a mockery of religion and the religious.

Religious pluralism or denial of religion in the garb of "different interpretations"

It is clear that what is presented today in our society as "different interpretations of religion" emanates from the second group. Although the abovementioned term is advanced by so-called Muslim intellectuals, the essence of the notion of "different interpretations of religion" must be sought in humanism or man-centeredness. As stated before, the said notion regards the religious accounts, ordinances and injunctions of heavenly scriptures as meaningless, and it holds that the Qur'an or any religious text is silent and lacks any meaning and concept; in fact, it is we humans, having our own preconceptions, who attribute our understanding and interpretation to religion and the Qur'an. Accordingly, the Qur'an has no message of its own and does not speak of any truth.

With the purpose of clarifying the nature of this thought and understanding the argument of its proponents on the "silence of religion" and the possibility of different interpretations, citing an example might prove useful.

Perhaps, everybody is more or less familiar with the Dīvān [collection of poetry] of Ḥāfiẓ[1] and the ghazals[2] and other poems of this great poet and prominent mystic. The different readings of the dīvān of Ḥāfiẓ and the poems of this great poet mean that the composer of these poems has not meant anything in the words and expressions used in poetry. He has only put meaningless words and expressions together in a rhythmical form and arranged them as empty frameworks but of course with a very elegant and attractive rhythm. That is, while having no meaning, purpose and intention in mind, the poet has recited them.

In accordance with the notion of different readings, it is said that the ghazals and other poems of Ḥāfiẓ are devoid of any meaning. By consulting the book for a specific purpose and mindset, everyone opens the book of Ḥāfiẓ and interprets the first poem in a page or a ghazal in a certain way. For example, one who has a patient and wishes for his recovery consults the book and understands from a ghazal that his patient will not get well. Another person who has a debt understands from the same ghazal that he will soon pay it. A third person who hopes for the return home of his loved one who is on a journey receives from it glad tidings of the return of his beloved. In general, everyone understands something from these words according to his mindset. In reality, it is the individuals who give the book of Ḥāfiz the power of speech. Everyone puts his own words in the mouth of Ḥāfiẓ and all interpretations, justifications and perceptions are considered correct because these understandings are those of individuals, while the expressions, words, ghazals, and other poems are assumed meaningless.

This notion is exactly the same as the "different interpretations of religion," which considers the Qur'an or any religious text meaningless and devoid of any message or significance. The proponents of this idea assume that the Qur'an does not state what to do or not to do, and what is true and correct or what is false and wrong. Rather, it is individuals who interpret truth and falsehood from the Qur'an, according to their own mindsets. Since these things originate from the minds of individuals, all of them can be considered correct. In fact, to judge them as correct or otherwise is meaningless because all different interpretations of a verse, though contradictory to one another, are considered correct. A person understands from a ghazal of

---

1 Khwājah Shams al-Dīn Muḥammad Ḥāfiẓ Shīrāzī (ca. 1325-1391) was the fourteenth century Persian lyric bard and panegyrist, and commonly considered as the preeminent master of the *ghazal* form. [Trans.]

2 *Ghazal* is a lyric form of Persian poetry, with rhyme in the first two and in even numbered lines, and allowing various metric forms. With respect to content, it usually does not express the linear development of an idea, but rather its couplets express variations on an idea or mood. [Trans.]

Ḥāfiz that his patient will get well. Another person learns from it that his loved one who is traveling will return soon. A third person becomes hopeless and expects the death of his patient.

The proponents of the notion of "different interpretations of religion" claim that the Qur'an or any religious text is also like that. They believe that individuals are not supposed to accuse one another of misunderstanding the Qur'an because understanding it does not require any expertise since the Qur'an or any religious text has no message of its own for it to be understood. The fact of the matter is that "understanding" is within the realm of man. In our opinion, the promotion of this idea is meant to attain certain political goals but it is outwardly advanced and promoted as a religious epistemological theory and called "new interpretation of religion," "straight paths," or the like. Religious pluralism which is presented in the framework of "different interpretations of religion" is not very logically or rationally substantiated. Once a rational person examines the roots of this idea and its effects, he will undoubtedly confirm its falsity and futility. On the other hand, given the destructive impacts of pluralist thought in religious society, it cannot easily be ignored.

It seems that coupled with thousands of years of experience, one of the most effective snares which Satan—this sworn enemy of mankind—has used since the creation of Ḥaḍrat Ādam (Adam) ('a) to deceive the worshippers of God and monotheists is to advance the notion of "different interpretations of religion". Inspired by this satanic thinking, so-called intellectuals rush to the help of Satan and exert all efforts to assist him in this regard. They have placed their talents and powers of oral and written expressions at the disposal of Satan and set themselves as instruments to misguide people.

We have to think as much as possible about the true meaning of "different interpretations of religion" or "straight paths" and to reflect on the destructive effects and repercussions of this atheistic thought so that we can find out the goals of the founders and proponents of this satanic snare and realize the intensity of their movement.

In any case, once we compare this tendency with that of the first group, [we will find out that] the spirit of the first tendency is God-centeredness or servitude and submission to God, the Exalted, and the spirit of the second tendency is man-centeredness or keeping away from God and His commandments. In the first tendency, the efforts are generally exerted for man to accept his servitude to God, the Exalted, while in the second tendency the efforts are exerted for man to deny his servitude to God and indulge in bestial inclinations and passions. This tendency sets human inclinations and desires as the essence and tries to interpret and justify religion or the Qur'an according to them.

Perhaps, one of the reasons behind the emphasis of the Qur'an on its descriptions such as ﴿ تِلْكَ آيَاتُ الْكِتَابِ وَقُرْآنٍ مُّبِينٍ ﴾ *"These are the signs of the Book and a manifest Qur'an,"*[1] ﴿ بِلِسَانٍ عَرَبِيٍّ مُّبِينٍ ﴾*"In a clear Arabic language,"*[2] ﴿ تِلْكَ آيَاتُ الْقُرْآنِ وَكِتَابٍ مُّبِينٍ ﴾ *"These are the signs of the Qur'an and a manifest Book,"*[3] and ﴿ قَدْ جَاءَكُم مِّنَ اللَّهِ نُورٌ وَكِتَابٌ مُّبِينٌ ﴾ *"Certainly there has come to you a light from Allah and a manifest Book,"*[4] which highlight the clarity, lucidity and expressiveness of the Qur'an is exactly to prevent deviant thoughts like "different interpretations of religion" and refute any allegation of ambiguity and vagueness in the meaning and purport of the Qur'an.

Thus, the Qur'an is the book of guidance in which God, the Exalted, has stated all the truths necessary for the happiness of man in this world and the hereafter. By reflecting on the Qur'an, Muslims are duty-bound to know their individual and social duties and guarantee their salvation by following it. Meanwhile, the question on who is the competent person to interpret the Qur'an and religious teachings is a subject which we shall now deal with.

The necessity of acquiring competence in understanding and interpreting the Qur'an

It is evident that not everyone can understand and interpret the Qur'an just as not everyone can understand subtle scientific facts in any field or domain. To understand complex mathematical equations or subtleties of other sciences is within the competence of the experts only, and the non-experts are not only incapable of expressing views in this regard but their views are devoid of any value whatsoever.

Concerning the Qur'an, the views of those who are not familiar with the religious sciences and teachings are devoid of any value and importance. It is true that the Qur'an has been revealed in a clear and eloquent language so that the people can understand and put it into practice, but it does not mean that the profundity of its knowledge [ma'ārif] can uniformly be grasped by one and all. What can be understood by the common people from the Qur'an is that level of meaning which the Qur'an itself mentions to the effect: "We revealed the Qur'an in plain language." That is, the Qur'an has been revealed in such a manner that anyone who knows Arabic and

---

1 *Sūrah al-Ḥijr* 15:1.

2 *Sūrah al-Shu'arā'* 26:195.

3 *Sūrah al-Naml* 27:1.

4 *Sūrah al-Mā'idah* 5:15.

possesses the spirit of servitude to God can understand it and benefit from it according to his own intellectual level. However, to fathom the meanings and knowledge [ma'ārif] of the Qur'an a great deal of reflection and thinking is needed. In this regard, the Qur'an says:

﴿ إِنَّا أَنزَلْنَاهُ قُرْآنًا عَرَبِيًّا لَّعَلَّكُمْ تَعْقِلُونَ ﴾

*"Indeed We have sent it down as an Arabic Qur'*an *so that you may apply reason."*[1]

﴿ إِنَّا جَعَلْنَاهُ قُرْآنًا عَرَبِيًّا لَّعَلَّكُمْ تَعْقِلُونَ ﴾

"We have made it an Arabic Qur'an so that you may apply reason."[2]

In general, the verses that invite mankind to reflect and apply reason regarding the Qur'an and its teachings tell us that we should not only depend on the outward meanings of the Qur'an. Instead, by relying upon reflection, reason and the knowledge of the Ahl al-Bayt ('a), we have to explore the profundity and subtleties of the Qur'an and benefit from this treasure of divine knowledge more than ever. Therefore, to understand the Qur'an and interpret its sublime knowledge [ma'ārif] is only within the competence of the experts who are acquainted with the knowledge of the Ahl al-Bayt ('a). A neophyte without any knowledge of religion and the principles and rules governing the exegesis [tafsīr] of the Qur'an, has no right to express a view or say anything under the name of a "new interpretation of religion and its laws and teachings".

Different degrees of meaning and understanding of Qur'anic concepts

Many traditions [aḥādīth] can be quoted as pointing towards the inner [bāṭin] and outer [ẓāhir] aspects of Qur'anic knowledge [ma'ārif], and not everyone is capable of discerning its depth. As stated before, the Qur'an is a deep and boundless ocean. Depending on one's capability and skill in diving, anyone can go searching for that oceanic jewel of knowledge, go further beyond the outward aspects [ẓawāhir], fathom its profound knowledge, and infer various facts of diverse meanings from a single verse without the minutest contradiction. This is in itself one of the miracles [mu'jizāt] of the Qur'an.

For instance, the Qur'an thus states:

---

1 *Sūrah Yūsuf* 12:2.

2 *Sūrah al-Zukhruf* 43:3.

﴿ يَا أَيُّهَا النَّاسُ أَنتُمُ الْفُقَرَاءُ إِلَى اللَّهِ وَاللَّهُ هُوَ الْغَنِيُّ الْحَمِيدُ ﴾

"O mankind! You are the ones who stand in need of Allah, and Allah is He who is the All-sufficient, the All-laudable."[1]

What common people understand from this verse as it outwardly indicates is that we are in need of God, the Exalted, who is self-sufficient and worthy of praise. By the word faqr [poverty], what come to the minds of common people are human needs for subsistence such as food, clothing and others. By creating their causes and effects, God, the Exalted, provides means for the subsistence, growth and evolution of man. At this level of understanding which is the "outward level," the Qur'an is clear and evident and all those who know its language can understand it well. It does not mean, however, that another meaning which is deeper than this outward meaning cannot be inferred from it and the abovementioned verse does not point to any fact more profound than what the common people understand. The more a person is acquainted with the different subjects of scholastic theology ['ilm al-kalām] and literary nuances of the Arabic language, the more he reflects and ponders on each verse, and finds subtler and more profound meanings than the obvious meanings of the Qur'an.

If we try to reflect a bit deeper on this verse, we will realize that our poverty and need for God, the Exalted, is beyond the need for food, clothing, health, and material things. We are in absolute poverty while God is All-sufficient. We are essentially poor [faqīr bi'dh-dhāt] while God is Self-sufficient in essence [ghanī bi'dh-dhāt]. Literally, "poor" refers to a person whose pillars of support are broken and he is incapable of standing. "Man is poor" means that even if all material things are provided for him, his existence is defective and dependent. The essence of our existence is in need of God. It is God, the Exalted, who has created us. By creating the causes and effects of existence, it is He who has provided the ground for man's subsistence, growth and evolution. By the nature and essence of our being, we are poor and needy while God is All-sufficient in essence.

It is evident that the second perspective is deeper than the first one. The first and second meanings are considered "outer" and "inner" respectively. And even more profound meaning than the second one is for us to say that human beings are not only poor and needy by the nature of their existence but by the nature of the very "need" itself. Their need for existence is their connection with God, the Exalted. Of course, to understand the truth of the third meaning is beyond the capability of common people.

1 *Sūrah Fāṭir* (or *al-Malā'ikah*) 35:15.

It must be noted that all three interpretations of this verse run parallel, all three are correct and rightful, none of them contradicts the other. In terms of depth, however, they are not of the same level. It is not correct to say that all degrees of the meanings of the Qur'an are universally understandable and that all people have the power and capability to understand all levels and degrees of the Qur'an. It is necessary to emphasize and point out that after the Apostle (*ṣ*), only the Imāms ('a), through divine inspiration, possess the knowledge and sciences of the Qur'an and are cognizant of the inner aspects of this great heavenly book. In this regard, we shall partially quote below a relevant tradition:

عَنْ أَبِي جَعْفَرٍ (ع) فَقَالَ يَا جَبِرْ! إِنَّ لِلْقُرْآنِ بَطْنًا وَلِلْبَطْنِ بَطْنٌ وَلَهُ ظَهْرٌ وَلِلظَّهْرِ ظَهْرٌ يَا جَابِرْ! وَلَيْسَ شَيْءٌ أَبْعَدُ مِنْ عُقُوْلِ الرِّجَالِ مِنْ تَفْسِيْرِ الْقُرْآنِ إِنَّ الْآيَةَ يَكُوْنُ أَوَّلُهَا فِي شَيْءٍ وَآخِرُهَا فِي شَيْءٍ وَهُوَ كَلَامٌ مُتَّصِلٌ يُتَصَرَّفُ عَلَىٰ وُجُوهٍ

> Abū Ja'far (Imām Muḥammad al-Bāqir) ('a) said: "O Jābir! The Qur'an has an interior [b*āṭ*in] and this interior is within an interior. It also has an exterior [*ẓā*hir] and this exterior is within an exterior. O Jābir! Also know that the intellects of men are incapable of interpreting the Qur'an. Verily, the first part of a verse may deal with a thing while its latter part may deal with another thing. It consists of words connected together with the capacity of having various meanings (though without being contradictory to one another)."[1]

What is emphasized here is that understanding the inner meanings and subtleties of the Qur'an is not within the competence of everybody. Of course, it does not mean that the Qur'an has been revealed only for the Imāms ('a) and scholars, and others are incapable of understanding even the outward meanings of the Qur'an. In fact, the outward meanings of the Qur'an can be beneficial to everyone, depending on the talent and the level of understanding and discernment, provided that he sets aside his prejudgment as well as carnal desires and inclinations, and avoids speculative interpretation. In connection with understanding the Qur'an, one has to pay special attention to certain points which we shall deal with under the following heading.

1 *Biḥār al-Anwār*, vol. 92, p. 91.

Confining the Apostle (ṣ) and infallible Imāms' ('a) interpretation of the Qur'an to the exposition of laws

As stated and proved in the pertinent section, one of the functions of the Apostle (ṣ) apart from receiving and conveying the revelation is to explain it and elucidate the divine laws and decrees. The Holy Qur'an has been revealed to the Apostle (ṣ) in the form of a set of general laws and ordinances whose details have not been explained elaborately except in a few cases. Their elaborate explanations have been assigned to the Apostle (ṣ) and thereafter the infallible Imāms ('a). For example, the Qur'an enjoins the ritual prayer [ṣalāt] in general terms and calls on the Muslims to establish prayers, but the procedure of its performance—the number of raka'āt [cycles or units], manner of recitation, and its conditions and details—have not been mentioned in the Qur'an. Elaborate exposition of these general laws and the like has been assigned to the Apostle (ṣ). Thus, the interpretation and elucidation of the divine laws has been assigned to the Apostle (ṣ) and it is one of his prophetic functions. The Qur'an also pays attention to the function of explaining the revelation and considers it as one of the duties of the Apostle (ṣ):

﴿ وَأَنزَلْنَا إِلَيْكَ الذِّكْرَ لِتُبَيِّنَ لِلنَّاسِ مَا نُزِّلَ إِلَيْهِمْ ﴾

"We have sent down the reminder to you so that you may clarify for the people that which has been sent down to them."[1]

It is likely that the purport of "teaching" in verses like āyah 164 of Sūrah Āl 'Imrān in which "teaching" is mentioned along with "recitation" also bespeaks of the position and function of the Apostle (ṣ) in elucidating and interpreting Qur'anic revelations.

In reality, while conveying the revelation, the Apostle (ṣ) had been performing two functions, viz. reciting the revealed words to the people, and elucidating and interpreting its meaning and purport to acquaint them with the laws and teachings of the Qur'an. In this regard, the Qur'an states:

﴿ لَقَدْ مَنَّ اللّهُ عَلَى الْمُؤمِنِينَ إِذْ بَعَثَ فِيهِمْ رَسُولاً مِّنْ أَنفُسِهِمْ يَتْلُو عَلَيْهِمْ آيَاتِهِ وَيُزَكِّيهِمْ وَيُعَلِّمُهُمُ الْكِتَابَ وَالْحِكْمَةَ وَإِن كَانُواْ مِن قَبْلُ لَفِي ضَلالٍ مُّبِينٍ ﴾

"Allah certainly favored the faithful when He raised up among them an apostle from among themselves to recite to them His signs and to

1 *Sūrah al-Naḥl* 16:44.

> *purify them, and to teach them the Book and wisdom, and earlier they had indeed been in manifest error."*[1]

In this and similar verses, the first duty has been mentioned with the phrase "to recite" [yatlū] and in mentioning the second duty the expression "to teach" [ta'līm] has been used.

In conclusion, elucidation of the revelation and elaborate explanation of the divine laws and exegesis of the Holy Qur'an in the above sense is a function which is only within the competence of the Apostle (ṣ) and the infallible Imāms ('a), for they are the only ones blessed with divine knowledge and wisdom by God.

Acquiring the knowledge provided by the Ahl al-Bayt ('a) as a prerequisite in understanding and interpreting the Qur'an

The duty of the exegetes [mufassirīn] becomes very clear. As pointed out before, elucidation of the revelation, elaborate explanation of the laws and interpretation of the Qur'anic verses are essentially assigned to and within the competence of the Apostle (ṣ) who, during his blessed life, acquainted the people whenever it was possible with the teachings of the Qur'an. Today, the exegetes are duty-bound to refer to the authentic traditions [aḥādīth] and narrations [riwāyāt] reported from the Apostle (ṣ) in this regard. Based on these traditions, they have to closely examine and scrutinize the relevant verses and organize their views and opinions within the framework of the Apostle's (ṣ) expositions and explanations. At the points where the Prophet (ṣ) did not have the opportunity to expound the Greater One of the Two Weighty Things [thiql al-akbar] i.e. the firm Qur'an, they have to resort to the Great One of the Two Weighty Things [thiql al-kabīr], viz. the Ahl al-Bayt ('a) and the infallible Imāms ('a). In this regard, the religious science experts and scholars are equally obliged to take the authentic traditions and narrations as their basis and proof in understanding the Holy Qur'an and base the exegesis or interpretation of the Qur'an on these traditions.

Therefore, the first criterion for correct understanding of the Qur'an and religious teachings is the elucidation or explanation transmitted from the Apostle (ṣ) and the infallible Imāms ('a) to us. Hence, the first and foremost duty of an exegete [mufassir] is to understand and expound the exegesis which has been reported from the Apostle (ṣ) and the Imāms ('a), for only in the light of the knowledge of the Ahl al-Bayt ('a) can one understand the sciences of the Qur'an.

---

1 *Sūrah Āl 'Imrān* 3:164.

Interpreting the Qur'an by means of the Qur'an

The third point which is extremely important and expedient to pay attention to in understanding correctly the revealed words is the issue of interpreting the Qur'an by means of itself and paying attention to the existing relationship between verses. It is true that the verses of the Qur'an are apparently separate from one another, and every verse or group of verses seemingly speaks about a specific subject, but correct understanding or proper interpretation is possible only when the verses of the Qur'an are taken into account in relation to one another. Many verses and points of this divine book interpret one another and give testimony to their veracity and truthfulness.

In this regard, Imām 'Alī ('a) says:

كِتَابُ اللهِ تُبْصِرُونَ بِهِ، وَتَنْطِقُونَ بِهِ، وَتَسْمَعُونَ بِهِ، وَيَنْطِقُ بَعْضُهُ بِبَعْضٍ، وَيَشْهَدُ بَعْضُهُ عَلَى بَعْضٍ، وَلاَ يَخْتَلِفُ فِي اللهِ، وَلاَ يُخَالِفُ بِصَاحِبِهِ عَنِ اللهِ

> "The Book of Allah is that through which you see, you speak and you hear. Its one part speaks for the other part, and one part testifies to the other. It does not create differences about Allah nor does it mislead its own follower from (the path of) Allah."[1]

Among the cases of the interpretation of the Qur'an by means of itself, one may cite for example *ā*yah 11 of S*ū*rah al-Shawr*ā* and *ā*yah 10 of S*ū*rah al-Fat*ḥ*:

﴿ لَيْسَ كَمِثْلِهِ شَيْءٌ وَهُوَ السَّمِيعُ الْبَصِيرُ ﴾

> *"Nothing is like Him, and He is the All-hearing, the All-seeing."*[2]

﴿ يَدُ اللَّهِ فَوْقَ أَيْدِيهِمْ ﴾

> *"The hand of Allah is above their hands."*[3]

"Nothing is like Him" is one of the precise verses [mu*ḥ*kam*ā*t] of the Qur'an and its meaning is clear and unambiguous. This verse states that nothing is like Him; that is, God, the Exalted, is the Unique Reality. The second verse states that "the hand of Allah is above their hands". It is true that this verse has attributed a "hand" to God but the first verse negates this apparent meaning and in view of which we can understand that by "yad" it does not

---

1 *Nahj al-Balāghah*, Sermon 133.

2 *Sūrah al-Shawrā* 42:11.

3 *Sūrah al-Fatḥ* 48:10.

suggest its apparent meaning, i.e. "hand". It rather refers to its allegorical meaning such as "power" and the like. Thus, interpreting and expounding the verse *"The hand of Allah is above their hands"* without paying attention to the verse "Nothing is like Him" is outside the periphery of proper method of interpretation and because of this wrong interpretation, it may possibly lead to the presentation of an erroneous anthropomorphic representation of God.

As such, in interpreting the Qur'an we have to pay attention to the verses in relation to one another and understand their meaning through the Qur'an itself.

Observing the principles and rules of intellectual discourse in understanding the Qur'an

The fourth point that must be noted in interpreting and correctly understanding the Qur'an is the observance of principles and rules of intellectual discourse. Especially when there is no available authentic tradition or clear explanation from the Apostle (ṣ) or the infallible Imāms ('a), the necessity of observing the principles and rules of intellectual discourse is multiplied. It is at this stage that the role of the prominent men of religion, exegetes and those who have acquired the knowledge of the Ahl al-Bayt ('a), becomes clear. They are the ones who in accordance with the principles of intellectual discourse identify the general ['*ām*] and specific [kh*āṣṣ*] injunctions of the Qur'an, specify the scope of meaning of each of them, know the abstract [mu*ṭ*laq] and concrete [muqayyad] meanings, interpret verses by means of one another, determine the precedence of one verse over another, and pay attention to them in their exegetical pursuits.

The understanding of exegetes commensurates with their competence

The other point which must be noted in this section is not confined to understanding the Qur'an and religious sciences. It is universally accepted that an individual's intellectual capabilities, extent of efforts exerted and meticulousness in correctly understanding a subject decide the degree of his understanding. Let us elaborate:

In juristic discussions, one of the issues which are more or less affirmed by all jurists [fuqah*ā*] and considered part of the duties of every follower [muqallid][1] is the question of following [taql*ī*d] the more knowledgeable or the most learned [a'lam]. Accordingly, it is said that expertise in

1 *Muqallid* (lit. imitator, emulator or follower): the person who follows a certain *marja' al-taqlīd* [source of emulation or reference authority] in matters of religious jurisprudence. [Trans.]

jurisprudence [fiqh] and the deduction of laws from religious sources [ijtihād] has various levels. Every mukallaf[1] is obliged to follow [taqlīd] the most learned jurist [faqīh], i.e. one who in matters of ijtihād has the superior understanding and talent and is the most knowledgeable in jurisprudence. Of course, the other marāji' al-taqlīd [sources of emulation or religious authorities] who are not equal to the most learned in matters of ijtihād are also fuqahā and mujtahidūn but they are on a lower level. It must not remain unsaid that the religious edict [fatwā] of the fuqahā on the necessity of following the most learned also stems from the rational method. It is exactly like referring to an expert doctor who has many years of medical experience. To prefer him over a doctor who has recently acquired his license to practice medicine is the rational decision, and to do otherwise is condemned by all rational people. Understanding and identifying the subtleties of the Qur'an is only within the competence of the experts who spent their lives understanding the Qur'an and religious sciences with the knowledge acquired from the Ahl al-Bayt ('a). Keeping in view the different degrees of understanding and interpreting this heavenly book, it is evident that the more the abovementioned points and affairs are taken into account, the lesser will be the probability of committing mistakes while interpreting the divine verses, and easier to get closer to the correct understanding of this heavenly scripture.

The necessity of paying attention to the linguistic contexts

The sixth point to which we would like to draw the attention of the readers is the necessity of paying attention to the linguistic and positional contexts and the occasion of the revelation of the verses. It is true that the Holy Qur'an has been revealed for all ages and generations and addressed to the people of all ages, but the context and occasion of revelation was clear for the first addressees and people of the period of revelation and there was no room for doubt and dispute on their meanings and interpretations. Moreover, if there was any ambiguity surrounding a verse, the people's access to the Apostle (ṣ) was not problematic. Today, however, the possibility of some contexts and occasions of revelations being concealed, the expediency or need for meticulousness in properly understanding the Qur'an becomes far more important.

On the other hand, information about the true and literal meanings of words used in the Holy Qur'an is one of the issues without which it is impossible to correctly understand and properly interpret the Qur'an. Negligence in the

1 *Mukallaf* (lit. charged with a duty): *comopos mentis* or adult person bound to observe the precepts of religion. [Trans.]

transformation of meanings, which sometimes happens in the course of time to a certain word, may possibly lead to error and misunderstanding.

For example, the meaning and concept of the word taqiyyah [dissimulation] is clear to all. In popular usage this word means that a person conceals his faith or religion and acts in such a manner that others are uninformed of his real faith or religion while the literal meaning of taqiyyah is piety and it has been used in the Qur'an and Nahj al-Balāghah in this sense. The word taqiyyah is not mentioned in the Qur'an but the word taqāh which is synonymous with taqiyyah and taqwā [piety or God-wariness] is mentioned in the passage below:

﴿ اتَّقُواْ اللّهَ حَقَّ تُقَاتِهِ ﴾

"Be wary of Allah with the wariness due to Him."[1]

The existence of literary beauties in the Holy Qur'an

It is true that the Holy Qur'an, as it declares itself, has been revealed in a clear and expressive language, and depending on the level of understanding and talent, one can benefit from this heavenly book, but it is worthy of note that the Qur'an possesses the most eloquent and expressive literary and rhetorical beauties. It is evident that paying attention to the abovementioned points is also one of the basic conditions of correctly and properly benefiting from the Holy Qur'an.

Sometimes, in the Holy Qur'an a certain verse mentions a decree in a general and common sense, and in another verse the limitation of the said decree is clarified. Or, in a certain verse a decree is stated in an absolute sense and its condition or requisite can be inferred from another verse. Elaborating a point by means of an example or the use of allusion, metaphor, allegory, and the like is also one of methods employed in the Qur'an. Since those who are addressed by the Qur'an are humans and the stated methods are considered among the beauties of human speech in expressing concepts and points, the Qur'an also uses the stated methods in the best possible manner while declaring its decrees and teachings. Therefore, the methods used in the Qur'an are the same methods used by the wise in expressing their intentions but with a difference. The art of expression in the Qur'an cannot be compared in terms of degree, beauty and eloquence with its use by man. The reason for this is that the Qur'an is the Word of God, the Exalted, which has been revealed to the Apostle (ṣ) in the most eloquent manner, and has taught the principles of eloquence and

1 *Sūrah Āl 'Imrān* 3:102.

fluency to mankind. This book has invited the people to monotheism, guidance, perfection, and felicity in the most beautiful and eloquent manner.

In a single statement: neglect of any of the above-mentioned prerequisites will lead to a misunderstanding and incorrect interpretation of the heavenly book—the Holy Qur'an. χ

Chapter 3

The Qur'an and the Cultural Onslaught

The contradictory nature of truth and falsehood

The status and importance of the Qur'an and the role of this divine book according to *Nahj al-Balāghah* in the guidance of mankind toward felicity and perfection has been explained briefly. The next important question that comes to mind is: Is it enough to observe the abovementioned points to benefit from the Holy Qur'an and cling to the *thiql al-akbar*—this great legacy of the Great Prophet (ṣ)? It might be concluded that if all the points necessary in correctly understanding the Qur'an are observed, the ordinances and teachings of the Qur'an will accurately be understood, the culture of society will be formed according to the instructions of the Holy Qur'an, and under the auspices of the religious government and the Qur'an, people will become immune from the threat of deviation. In the guidance of individuals, this answer is to some extent correct but comprehensive guidance can only be achieved when this is done on the macro level. It is clear that without knowing the deviant ideas of the enemies of the Qur'an and thwarting their cultural conspiracies through enlightenment, it would be extremely difficult to establish the culture of the Qur'an and guide society according to its religious beliefs and values. This is the area which is usually neglected.

Truth and falsehood clash in the realm of practice just as they do in the realm of theory. Once truth is identified, falsehood will also be identified, and knowing falsehood also helps you know the truth. Similarly, in the realm of practice, making the Qur'an reign supreme in society is not possible without knowing the enemies and combating their satanic plots and schemes against the religious culture of the people. In this regard, we shall first pay attention to the statement of Ḥaḍrat 'Alī (*'a*) recorded in *Nahj al-Balāghah*. Then, we will acquaint the masses, especially the youth and the educated with the satanic stratagems of the opponents of the Qur'an to mislead the people.

Ḥaḍrat 'Alī (*'a*) said:

وَاعْلَمُوا أَنَّكُمْ لَنْ تَعْرِفُوا الرُّشْدَ حَتَّى تَعْرِفُوا الَّذِي تَرَكَهُ، وَلَنْ تَأْخُذُوا بِمِيثَاقِ الْكِتَابِ حَتَّى تَعْرِفُوا الَّذِي نَقَضَهُ، وَلَنْ تَمَسَّكُوا بِهِ حَتَّى تَعْرِفُوا الَّذِي نَبَذَهُ فَالْتَمِسُوا ذلِكَ مِنْ عِنْدِ أَهْلِهِ، فَإِنَّهُمْ عَيْشُ الْعِلْمِ، وَمَوْتُ الْجَهْلِ

> "You should know that you will never know guidance unless you know who has abandoned it, you will never abide by the pledges of the Qur'an unless you know who has broken them, and will never cling to it unless you know who has forsaken it. Seek these things from those who own them because they are the life spring of knowledge and death of ignorance."[1]

This instructive statement of Ḥaḍrat 'Alī (*'a*) on the need to know the enemies and identify their deviant ideas renders the burden of responsibility of the religious scholars, preachers and propagators much heavier. Purging the minds of the people, especially the youth, who do not have sufficient knowledge of religion, of the objections and doubts of the atheists is one of the fundamental tasks of propagation and promotion of Qur'anic or religious culture, without which one cannot expect a desirable result. To make this matter clear, we shall deal with this subject in three sections: the doubts, the approach, and the motive of the enemies in instilling the doubts.

It is true that the Qur'an is the greatest favor that God, the Exalted, has ever granted His servants and He Himself has guaranteed its protection and preservation from distortion by the wicked, but this is not the end of the story. At every moment, depending on the condition and spiritual state of those who in terms of social status are capable of exerting influence on the minds of people, Satan, the sworn enemy of the Children of Adam, instills doubts into their minds so as to draw the masses of people towards him and away from the Qur'an and religion. Since the Qur'an is the greatest means of guidance, salvation and felicity of mankind, the main goal of Satan is to separate human beings from the Qur'an and religion. One of the means used by Satan along this way is to instill doubts about religion or the Qur'an to weaken the faith of the people.

---

1 *Nahj al-Balāghah*, Sermon 147.

The activities of Satan and his human entourage in suppressing the Qur'an have been there since its revelation. They started with the closing of ears and refusing to listen to the divine verses, followed by impugning and calumniating the Prophet (*ṣ*). They continue today in various forms and will continue in future. In this regard, we shall cite only some of the doubts expressed in society today, and try to clear the minds of readers so that by becoming aware of their satanic stratagems, they can confront the cultural onslaught of the enemies.

As the devils failed to destroy and annihilate the Qur'an in their campaign against it, they decided to deprive the people of getting acquainted with its content. For many centuries the enemies of the Qur'an propagated among the Muslims, the Shī'ah in particular, that the Qur'an is beyond their understanding and they have no knowledge of its esoteric aspect. As such, one cannot rely only upon its exoteric aspect. By promoting this idea, they tried to deprive people of the benefits of the Qur'an and remove it from the lives of Muslims. It is true that the outward respect to the Qur'an in the form of reciting and kissing it and considering it holy remained among Muslims, but they were deprived of its content and discouraged from putting its divine instructions into practice.

Nowadays, so-called intellectuals who have scanty knowledge of the Islamic sciences instill the most deceiving doubts—used in the past centuries in the West against the distorted scriptures of other religions—under the rubric of "new thinking" among the cultural and academic circles and influence the educated class who are uninformed of their false ideas and satanic imagination. They are doing so with the hope of undermining the foundation of beliefs of this class without knowing that the Muslims, especially the educated ones with inquisitive minds, soon realize the falsity of their baseless, fictitious, illogical, and irrational ideas. The beliefs of the Muslims and religious scholars are anchored in logic and rationality, derived from the knowledge of the Apostle (*ṣ*) and the infallible Imāms (*'a*) and stem from the fountain of divine revelation. Whenever a Muslim comes across with deviant ideas in the intellectual and ideological domain, he refers to experts and scholars of the religious sciences so as to receive the logical and correct answer.

The alleged inaccessibility of the truth of religion

The alleged "inaccessibility of the truth of religion" has been advanced with extremely wicked motives and far-reaching destructive effects, but presently it will suffice to explain the nature of this doubt and explicitly mention some of its hidden dimensions and properties, and leave the judgment to you.

Since our discussion pertains to the Holy Qur'an, we shall examine and discuss the abovementioned doubt or misgiving in relation to it. This doubt is raised in various forms on different levels. Sometimes, it is claimed that some verses of the Holy Qur'an have diverse interpretations on which the exegetes do not have a consensus of opinion. No matter how we research to arrive at the correct view, at the end we will accept the interpretation and opinion of one of the exegetes, which other exegetes do not regard as the view of the Qur'an. It is therefore impossible to obtain the real view of the Qur'an.

By doing so, the promoters of this misgiving unsurprisingly want to instill doubt into the minds of those who are mentally weak and do not have sufficient knowledge of religious sciences to analyze and respond. The skeptics think that the intellectual and ideological foundations of Muslims are based upon blind following. They know that whenever there is talk about thought, reason and logic, only the Qur'an, along with its teachings is affirmed by a sound mind and correct logic, and wholeheartedly accepted by every truth-seeking person. They then try to raise this doubt in a more profound way so that they can render a severer blow to religious thought, without realizing that by scrutinizing their ideas Muslim thinkers will discover that this type of idea leads to nothing but the abyss of skepticism.

In any case, it can be inferred from the way this doubt is expressed that the promoters believe that the Holy Qur'an has immutable truths but since the exegetes do not have a consensus of opinion on the exegesis of the Qur'an, we are incapable of stating the truth of the Qur'an. It is therefore impossible to benefit from the Qur'an and it must be set aside.

But when they are confronted with explicit and categorical verses of the Qur'an and cannot find fault with the unambiguous verses nor refute its reasoning and precise verses, they express the doubt in a different manner. They totally withdraw from their former stance on the alleged impossibility of understanding the Qur'an and religious knowledge and assume the diametrically opposite stance. They regard the Qur'an and religious accounts as devoid of any reality, and religious ordinances and precepts as human beings' theoretical understandings of Qur'anic verses. They claim that not only the Qur'an but all religious scriptures have been sent down so that they may be interpreted in diverse ways, and all these different interpretations and various understandings are correct and right. If it is asked, "Is it so even if these interpretations and understandings are contradictory to each other?" they will reply that the diversity of interpretations, even if conflicting, does not create any problem, because in essence, the Qur'an has never stated any reality. Rather, mere empty words and frameworks under the guise of "divine revelation" have been imparted to the Prophet (ṣ), and by consulting them everyone can deduce anything from them! What is actually presented is mere human understanding, and since humans have different mentalities, their interpretations may vary from one another. Religion is nothing but diverse human understanding of the words and verses of the Qur'an and religious accounts, and since they do not represent any reality, diverse interpretations cannot also be confirmed or falsified. All interpretations reveal the truth and must be deemed correct and right because the Qur'an does not state immutable truths which are consistent with only one of these interpretations.

The founders of the theory of "straight paths" or "different interpretations of religion" have gone further. In a bid to strike a blow to the basis and foundation of religion, i.e. divine revelation, they assert that not only can human beings not discern immutable truths from the Qur'an or divine revelation, and that everyone expresses and interprets what is in his mind as "revelation", but even the Apostle (ṣ), because of his being human, has expressed his understanding and interpretation as "revelation" to the people. Accordingly, the understanding of the Apostle (ṣ) has also been a personal one in accordance with his mentality and the circumstances of his time and place and has been expressed in the form of words and verses. As such, it is asserted that the Qur'an cannot be considered the Word of God and divine revelation. Instead, it must be said that the Qur'an is the word of the Prophet (ṣ).

Definitely, you will ask: what can we say about the verses quoted below?

﴿ وَمَا يَنطِقُ عَنِ الْهَوَى * إِنْ هُوَ إِلاَّ وَحْيٌ يُوحَى ﴾

> *"He does not speak out of [his own] desire: it is just a revelation that is revealed [to him]."*[1]

﴿تَنزِيلٌ مِن رَبِّ الْعَالَمِينَ * وَلَوْ تَقَوَّلَ عَلَيْنَا بَعْضَ الْأَقَاوِيلِ * لَأَخَذْنَا مِنْهُ بِالْيَمِينِ * ثُمَّ لَقَطَعْنَا مِنْهُ الْوَتِينَ﴾

> *"[It is] gradually sent down from the Lord of all the worlds. Had he faked any sayings in Our name, We would have surely seized him by the right hand and then cut off his aorta."*[2]

The proponents of this theory say in reply that these points are also the understanding or interpretation of the Prophet (ṣ) and represent his feelings.

It is evident that such theories lead to nothing but skepticism, denial of reality, disregard for logical reasoning, and playing with words. In dealing

---

1 *Sūrah al-Najm* 53:3-4.

2 *Sūrah al-Ḥā*qqah 69:40-47.

with the most explicit meanings and unambiguous concepts, the promoters of this theory say, "This is your feeling and interpretation which does not indicate any truth except your own personal opinion. Hence, it is good and respectable for you but for others it has no value at all!"

The promotion of such notions about religion and the Qur'an is one of the most advanced stratagems and snares of Satan which have so far been used to deceive and beguile the Children of Adam.

Inculcation and repetition as a key weapon of the devils

One of the stratagems of the devils in beguiling human beings is their persistence and determination to influence minds. For this reason, the Qur'an describes them as "sneaky tempters" [*al-waswāsi'l-khannās*] and instructs people to seek the protection of God from the evil of the devils from among the jinn and humans,[1] for by incessant inculcation and repetition of false notions, they want to place them under the sphere of their influence and misguide them.

The devils from among the jinn and humans know that in order to inculcate satanic notions in the minds of God-worshipping people, they have to speak and write a lot so as to accustom minds with their false notions and exert constant influence. They admit that they have to speak and write a lot so that the people finally entertain doubt and uncertainty.

By taking inspiration from Iblīs (Satan), their priority is to beguile and mislead the professional and educated class, for they believe that by deceiving them they can mislead the masses with greater ease, without realizing that God, the Exalted, has set plenty of torches for the guidance of Muslims who, by divine grace will unravel the satanic stratagems of the enemies and become firmer and more determined to follow the Qur'an.

Citing the allegorical verses [mutashābihāt] of the Qur'an as another way of confronting the Qur'an

It was stated earlier that one of the functions of the Apostle (*ṣ*) and the infallible Imāms (*'a*) is to interpret and expound divine revelation, for the Qur'an has precise [*muḥkamāt*] and allegorical [*mutashābihāt*] verses, and as mentioned before, it has an interior [*bāṭin*] and exterior [*ẓāhir*]. It is impossible for anyone except the Apostle (*ṣ*), the infallible Imāms (*'a*) and those who have access to divine knowledge to fathom the depth of its knowledge, and none can interpret and expound it except those who seek knowledge through the school of the *Ahl al-Bayt* (*'a*).

---

1 See *Sūrah al-Nās* 114:1-6. [Trans.]

Therefore, according to the rational way of the ignorant referring to learned, there is no way of understanding the Qur'an and religious precepts except by referring to the Transmitter (*ṣ*) of this divine book and the infallible Imāms (*'a*) and the students of their school. Yet, not all people follow the rational way and are faithful to reason and the logical principles of understanding [*fahm*], instruction [*tafhīm*] and comprehension [*tafahhum*]. They are those whose only pursuit is the misguidance of people and whose sole aim is to instill doubt and create sedition [*fitnah*] in society. The Qur'an has also predicted this reality:

﴿ هُوَ الَّذِيَ أَنزَلَ عَلَيْكَ الْكِتَابَ مِنْهُ آيَاتٌ مُّحْكَمَاتٌ هُنَّ أُمُّ الْكِتَابِ وَأُخَرُ مُتَشَابِهَاتٌ فَأَمَّا الَّذِينَ فِي قُلُوبِهِمْ زَيْغٌ فَيَتَّبِعُونَ مَا تَشَابَهَ مِنْهُ ابْتِغَاء الْفِتْنَةِ وَابْتِغَاء تَأْوِيلِهِ وَمَا يَعْلَمُ تَأْوِيلَهُ إِلاَّ اللّهُ وَالرَّاسِخُونَ فِي الْعِلْمِ يَقُولُونَ آمَنَّا بِهِ كُلٌّ مِّنْ عِندِ رَبِّنَا وَمَا يَذَّكَّرُ إِلاَّ أُوْلُواْ الألْبَابِ ﴾

"It is He who has sent down to you the Book. Parts of it are definite verses, which are the mother of the Book, while others are metaphorical. As for those in whose hearts is deviance, they pursue what is metaphorical in it, courting temptation and courting its interpretation. But no one knows its interpretation except Allah and those firmly grounded in knowledge; they say, 'We believe in it; all of it is from our Lord.' And none takes admonition except those who possess intellect."[1]

The *muḥkamāt* of the Qur'an refer to the verses whose meanings are clear and whose contents are undeniable. The verses constitute the principles and quintessence of Qur'anic knowledge. The criterion and basis of the correctness or incorrectness of "religious knowledge" are the *muḥkamāt* or "the mother of the Book". On the contrary, there are verses which cannot be understood without the assistance of the *muḥkamāt* and not everybody can fathom the depth of their meanings. These verses are called "allegorical" verses [*mutashābihāt*].

The Qur'an has forbidden the people to follow the *mutashābihāt* without paying attention to the *muḥkamāt* and the exegesis and exposition of the Apostle (*ṣ*) and the infallible Imāms (*'a*). The Holy Qur'an regards the act of following the *mutashābihāt* as a sign of deviation of the heart, stating that those who take the *mutashābihāt* of the Qur'an as the basis of their thinking, understanding and beliefs are looking for sedition, speculative interpretation [*ta'wīl*] and distortion [*taḥrīf*] of the Qur'an. According to the Qur'an, none knows the interpretation and exegesis of the allegorical verses except God and "those firmly grounded in knowledge". "Those firmly grounded in

1 *Sūrah Āl 'Imrān* 3:7.

ose who have wholeheartedly acknowledged their g: "We believe in the Qur'an—both its definitive and ntirety comes from God."

he existence of allegorical verses [*mutashābihāt*] in

At this p possibly be asked: Why has the Qur'an not been revealed in such a manner that all its verses are evident, definitive, complete, and unambiguous so that all of them can be understood and grasped by everybody?

In reply to this question, some preliminary factors need to be pointed out. The minds of common human beings like us follow natural factors. When common human beings are born, they are first acquainted with tangible and material things through the senses, and their understanding and perception is confined to them. However, the mental power of man gradually becomes stronger and acquires the power of abstraction. Finally, he acquires the power of perceiving allegorical truths. The stronger man's intellect and power of abstraction are and the further he goes beyond the material realm, the better he can perceive allegorical realities. Since all human beings are not equal in terms of intellectual growth, they are also not identical in terms of perceiving intangible things. There are many cases when the level of understanding and perception of a 10-year child is still like that of a seven or eight-year old and even later he may possibly think of God and abstract things in the framework of time and space. It is because his understanding and talent as well as the power of thinking are still within the bounds of material things while the foundation of religion is faith in the unseen; that is, faith in abstract and immaterial realities. In this regard, the Qur'an states:

﴿ ذَلِكَ الْكِتَابُ لاَ رَيْبَ فِيهِ هُدًى لِلْمُتَّقِينَ * الَّذِينَ يُؤْمِنُونَ بِالْغَيْبِ ﴾

> *"This is the Book; there is no doubt in it, a guidance to the God-wary, who believe in the Unseen."*[1]

The foundation of faith, therefore, lies in belief in intangible realities. But the truth or essence of these realities is something which can not be understood except through divine inspiration to the apostles and infallible Imāms (*'a*). There is no way for us common human beings to perceive metaphysical truths and realities except by strengthening our rational power and gradually rising from the tangible to the abstract and metaphysical realities.

---

1 *Sūrah al-Baqarah* 2:2-3.

On the other hand, most of the words used in the abstract sense are originally used with tangible meanings. Take for example the following verses:

﴿ يَدُ اللَّهِ فَوْقَ أَيْدِيهِمْ ﴾

"The hand of Allah is above their hands."[1]

﴿ وَهُوَ الْعَلِيُّ الْعَظِيمُ ﴾

"And He is the All-exalted, the All-supreme."[2]

The words *fawq*, *'alī*, *'ālī*, and *'uluww* all mean "high" as opposed to "low". It is evident that at the beginning man could not understand any meaning of these words beyond the tangible. For example, man takes his head as the criterion for what is "high" and regards his feet as "low". He considers whatever is below his feet as "low". For this reason, it is said that the sky is "high" while the earth is "low" or "below". However, with his entrance into social life, he goes beyond these meanings and gradually perceives intangible and abstract meanings. That is, when it is said that so-and-so occupies a high position or is promoted to a higher position, man no longer understands "high" or "higher" in its tangible sense.

Obviously, in this kind of usage the intended meaning has become abstract. When it is said that "The One who has created all things by His will has an extremely high status," the highness attributed to God is infinitely above the highness attributed to an office head in relation to his subordinates. The distance between the two is the distance between zero and infinity, as well as that of real and virtual, for any highness or delegated position is false and perishable expect the Real Highness which is due and belongs to God, the Creator of the universe.

﴿ إِنَّمَا أَمْرُهُ إِذَا أَرَادَ شَيْئًا أَنْ يَقُولَ لَهُ كُنْ فَيَكُونُ ﴾

"When He wills something, all He needs to do is say to it, 'Be,' then it is."[3]

Therefore, when the Qur'an states, *"He is the All-exalted, the All-supreme,"*[4] it implies that neither the Highness of God is physical and tangible nor His Magnificence and Greatness have any material and

---

1 *Sūrah al-Baqarah* 2:255; *Sūrah al-Fatḥ* 48:10.

2 *Sūrah al-Shawrā* 42:4.

3 *Sūrah Yā-Sīn* 36:82.

4 *Sūrah al-Baqarah* 2:255; *Sūrah al-Fatḥ* 48:10.

corporeal connotation. But the truth behind the Magnificence and Greatness of God is something which is beyond human comprehension. Of course, in many cases there is no word which can be used in an intangible sense. So, there is no option but to use the same word and give an abstract meaning to it. For example, it is said that God is High and Great. "High" is the same word used to refer to the roof in relation to the floor. "Great" is also the same word used when describing Mount Damāvand.[1] Yet, when these words are used to describe God, their meanings become abstract. Again, their becoming abstract in meaning does not mean that their true sense, when applied to God, can be comprehended.

It is said that words which get closer to their true meanings through the above way are of the same type of similitude which elicits ambiguity and fallacy. When it is said that "God is above," one who has not yet been able to separate the above meanings from their tangible properties and attributes thinks that God is in heaven, although He is not a body to occupy space:

﴿ فَأَيْنَمَا تُوَلُّوا۟ فَثَمَّ وَجْهُ اللَّهِ ﴾

"So whichever way you turn, there is the face of Allah!"[2]

But he cannot comprehend it. Of course, he does not have any duty beyond what he can comprehend for he has no power beyond it.

When it is said, "Verily, Allah is the All-exalted, the All-supreme," one who goes beyond this stage, has more power of understanding and also comprehends delegated meanings, thinks that the Highness and Greatness of God is also like that of a head office in relation to his subordinates. But these two are actually cheese and chalk apart!

One who has spent his life seeking knowledge, wisdom and comprehension of abstract meanings understands an even higher meaning of exaltedness and greatness, saying that God has Essential Greatness in relation to others.

All the creatures exist and so does God, but the existence of God, the Blessed and Exalted, in terms of the existential level of greatness, cannot be compared with His creatures. But, again, the truth behind His Highness, Greatness and sublime level of existence is something which everyone can discern depending on his power of discernment although comprehending its essence is impossible for anyone. Now, keeping in view the above

---

1 With a height of 5,670 m, Mount Damāvand which is located near Tehran is the loftiest peak of Alborz Mountains, a mountain range in northern Iran, extending along the southern shore of the Caspian Sea. [Trans.]

2 *Sūrah al-Baqarah* 2:115.

explanation, we argue that whenever God wishes to tell us human beings something which is beyond our common understanding, He has to use words which we can comprehend to some extent after reflection, although it is beyond our comprehension to understand its essence. In such cases, there is no option but to use allegorical words.

As such, the verses which indicate metaphysical points and beyond the understanding of common human beings will more or less have certain degrees of metaphor, and whose essence can be known by the help of precise verses. For instance, whenever the Qur'an states, *"And He is the All-exalted, the All-supreme,"*[1] and we cannot comprehend the truth or essence of the greatness and exaltedness of the Supreme Being, we have to interpret it through precise verses such as *"Nothing is like Him"*[2] so as to avoid misunderstanding and misinterpretation. The first verse states that God is Exalted and Great while the second one informs us that He has no equal and partner. That is, whatever state of greatness and exaltedness we think of it is still below His true Greatness and Exaltedness because He is above that.

The same is true with respect to the Attributes of God. When it is said that God is All-knowing and All-powerful, it is clear that the essence of knowledge in relation to God is above that which is applied to human beings. But the truth of the Attributes of God is something which is incomprehensible for anyone except God whose Essence is His Knowledge, Life and Power.

For the guidance of man towards Him and His Attributes, God, the Exalted, has used the same words which man initially understands in their tangible senses so that man does not remain deprived of that lofty knowledge, no matter how imperfect.

Hence, the existence of allegorical verses in the Qur'an is part of divine wisdom, for without them, the means to comprehend abstract and intangible concepts and facts would be totally lost. But to cite, interpret and expound the allegorical verses, as stated earlier, is something that must be done by the help of precise verses. But not all individuals who intend to understand the Qur'an and its sciences would choose the abovementioned logical, rational and natural way of understanding divine knowledge. In the verse under discussion, God mentions the existence of definitive and allegorical verses in the Qur'an and says that *"Those in whose hearts is deviance"*[3] have some psychological and moral sickness. In other words, *"There is a*

1 *Sūrah al-Shawrā* 42:4.

2 *Sūrah al-Shawrā* 42:11.

3 *Sūrah Āl 'Imrān* 3:7.

sickness in their hearts."[1] They take the allegorical verses as the basis of their thinking and action. Without taking into account the precise verses of the Qur'an, they give preference to allegorical verses and thus pave the ground for their own and others' misguidance.

Amalgamation of truth and falsehood as another weapon of the deviators

Naturally, those who want to oppose religion, the Qur'an, religious values and precepts in Islamic society will never adopt the way of direct confrontation to achieve their objectives. It is because they know that, in doing so, they will face massive opposition from the Muslims and be defeated at the very start. Following psychological tips, they choose the appropriate approaches to achieve their satanic objectives.

One of their approaches is the amalgamation of truth with falsehood. They fuse elements of truth and falsehood in a beautiful manner so that their addressees who occasionally do not have sufficient knowledge and expertise in distinguishing truth from falsehood accept their words as a whole. As such, the false point embellished with the luster of truth and hidden under the veil of elegant literary expression gets unconsciously instilled in the minds of listeners.

Ḥaḍrat 'Alī (*'a*) said:

فَلَوْ أَنَّ الْبَاطِلَ خَلَصَ مِنْ مِزَاجِ الْحَقِّ لَمْ يَخْفَ عَلَى الْمُرْتَادِينَ، وَلَوْ أَنَّ الْحقَّ خَلَصَ مِنْ لَبْسِ الْبَاطِلِ انْقَطَعَتْ عَنْهُ أَلْسُنُ الْمُعَانِدِينَ، وَلكِن يُؤْخَذُ مِنْ هذَا ضِغْثٌ، وَمِنْ هذَا ضِغْثٌ، فَيُمْزَجَانِ! فَهُنَالِكَ يَسْتَوْلِي الشَّيْطَانُ عَلَى أَوْلِيَائِهِ، وَيَنْجُو الَّذِينَ سَبَقَتْ لَهُمْ مِنَ اللهِ الْحُسْنَى

> "If wrong had been pure and unmixed, it would not be hidden from those who are in search of it. And if right had been pure without admixture of wrong, those who bear hatred towards it would have been silenced. What is, however, done is that something is taken from here and something from there and the two are mixed! At this stage Satan overpowers his friends, and they alone escape for whom virtue has been apportioned by Allah from before."[2]

Naturally, the deviators and those whose hearts are in deviance, as described by the Qur'an, and are not willing to submit to God, take the allegorical verses and the group of traditions which are adulterated in terms of the chain of transmission [*san*ad], or metaphors in terms of content, as the

---

1 *Sūrah al-Baqarah* 2:10.

2 *Nahj al-Balāghah*, Sermon 50.

frontispiece of their propaganda activities against Islam. Meanwhile, they abhor listening to the precise verses of the Qur'an, the statements of truth and divine knowledge authentically transmitted from the *Ahl al-Bayt* or infallible Imāms (*'a*).

They who sometimes regard themselves as Muslims are knowingly or unknowingly in tandem with the enemies of Islam, for they are looking for negative points to be falsely attributed to Islam. By magnifying these negative points, they aim at undermining the inclination towards Islam of those truth-seeking individuals who have not yet embraced Islam. In this book, we are dealing not only with atheists and non-Muslim enemies but also with those who claim to be Muslims.

In order to refuse to listen to the words of truth and submit to reason and logic, they make justifications for themselves such as those mentioned in the section about "different readings and interpretations of religion", and maintain their stance without considering the implications of their statements. In this part, I shall let the dear readers themselves judge those justifications and their effects. However, out of sympathy and concern, we invite them to reexamine their faith, just as the Qur'an urges the faithful to invite one another to thinking, reflection, reform, and guidance, and remind one another of the truth

﴿ يَا أَيُّهَا الَّذِينَ آمَنُوا اسْتَجِيبُوا لِلَّهِ وَلِلرَّسُولِ إِذَا دَعَاكُم لِمَا يُحْيِيكُمْ ﴾

"O you, who have faith! Answer Allah and the Apostle when he summons you to that which will give you life."[1]

"Different interpretations" as a weapon in confronting the Qur'an

It should by now be clear that the said idea which is expressed under the name of "straight paths," the expression "different understandings, readings or interpretations of religion," or within the theoretical framework of "the language of religion" or "minimalist or maximalist religion" has no agenda but to oppose the religious beliefs of monotheist thought. Let them know that the wary Muslim scholars are smart enough to detect the illogical and irrational nature of their arguments and more than aware of the hidden agenda of the promoters of these groundless misgivings.

Motives of the opponents of religious culture according to the Qur'an

Keeping in view our discussions, this question can be asked: What is the motive of the opponents of the Qur'an and religious culture behind these

---

1 *Sūrah al-Anfāl* 8:24.

wicked acts? In reply, we shall first examine the view of the Qur'an and then explain the statement of Ḥaḍrat 'Alī (*'a*) in *Nahj al-Balāghah* in this regard.

It can be inferred from the Qur'an that since the very beginning of revelation, Satan has tried his best, by exploiting the weaknesses of the jinn and humans, to separate the people from the Qur'an. Other than this, nothing could be expected from Satan, for he swore:

﴿ فَبِعِزَّتِكَ لَأُغْوِيَنَّهُمْ أَجْمَعِينَ * إِلاَّ عِبَادَكَ مِنْهُمُ الْمُخْلَصِينَ ﴾

"By Your might, I will surely pervert them, except Your exclusive servants among them."[1]

In order to execute his plan of misguiding people and depriving them of the knowledge of the Qur'an, he made the precise verses a pretext. He encouraged or urged the materialists and his friends to follow the allegorical verses of the Qur'an without paying attention to its precise verses, so that through them he could also draw the rest towards uncertainty and doubt. After dividing the verses of the Qur'an into *muḥk*amāt and mutashābihāt, God, the Exalted, states:

﴿ فَأَمَّا الَّذِينَ فِي قُلُوبِهِمْ زَيْغٌ فَيَتَّبِعُونَ مَا تَشَابَهَ مِنْهُ ابْتِغَاءَ الْفِتْنَةِ وَابْتِغَاءَ تَأْوِيلِهِ ﴾

"As for those in whose hearts is deviance, they pursue what is metaphorical in it, courting temptation and courting its interpretation."[2]

His followers assist him in attaining his objective. The Qur'an describes these individuals as *"Those in whose hearts is deviance"* and *"Those in whose hearts is a sickness"* and forbids people from following them.

Our concern here is to explain from the Qur'anic perspective the motive of such individuals in their opposition to religious culture. The Holy Qur'an states that those who, with the intention of "courting temptation", take the allegorical verses as the basis of their thinking and actions, or abandon the exterior [*ẓāhir*] of the Qur'an under the pretext of the *mutashābihāt,* are sedition-mongers.

The question which is posed here is: what is sedition [*fitnah*] and sedition-mongering? The lexicographers, especially those who strive to look for the original meaning of the word and give meanings to words while keeping their root-words in view, have said that *fitnah* originally means "heating a

1 *Sūrah Ṣād* 38:82-83.

2 *Sūrah Āl 'Imrān* 3:7.

thing by means of fire". Whenever a thing is placed over a fire to be warmed, burned or melted, the Arabs say "It made the thing hot" [*fatanahu*]. In the Qur'an, the phrase *fatanahu* has also been used in its literal sense when it says:

﴿ يَوْمَ هُمْ عَلَى النَّارِ يُفْتَنُونَ ﴾

"It is the day when they will be tormented in the Fire."[1]

Therefore, the essence of the literal meaning of *fatanahu* is to burn and melt. However, as lexicographers say, the requisite of a literal meaning becomes the second or third meaning of the word. The same is true in the case of the word *fitnah*. As stated, *fitnah* originally means "to grow hot" but "to grow hot" has a requisite and that is if this growing hot or getting burned happens to a man—such as the verse *"It is the day when they will be tormented in the Fire"*—he will be in a state of agitation [*iḍṭirāb*]. Agitation is the outward condition of one who is physically burned. At times, it is an inner or spiritual state. As such, agitation is actually one of the requisites of *fitnah* or growing hot, and considering the expansion of the meaning of a word, *fitnah* also refers to the things that cause inner or spiritual agitation. Since a part of the inner or spiritual agitation is the worry or uncertainty in matters of beliefs, whatever causes such agitation is also called *fitnah*.

There is the term "sedition [*fitnah*] in religion" because by instilling superstitious or false notions, some individuals wish to create agitation or uncertainty in the conviction or faith of the faithful, and let them abandon the religion of truth.

An examination or test is also called *fitnah* for it causes agitation and worry. Since at the time of an examination a person is worried about the result, he has no peace of mind. In the Qur'an, the word *fitnah*, in the sense of agitation on account of a test, can be found in numerous verses. The Qur'an states:

﴿ أَنَّمَا أَمْوَالُكُمْ وَأَوْلَادُكُمْ فِتْنَةٌ ﴾

"Your possessions and children are only a test."[2]

It also says:

﴿ وَنَبْلُوكُم بِالشَّرِّ وَالْخَيْرِ فِتْنَةً ﴾

"And We will test you with good and ill by way of test."[1]

---

1 *Sūrah al-Dhāriyāt* 51:13.

2 *Sūrah al-Anfāl* 8:28.

Sometimes, the punishment or inconvenience itself is also referred to as *fitnah*.

It is evident that in the verse under discussion—*"It is He who has sent down to you the Book. Parts of it are precise verses, which are the mother of the Book, while others are allegorical. As for those in whose hearts is deviance, they pursue what is allegorical in it, courting temptation [fitnah]"*[2]—*fitnah* implies "sedition in religion", for following the *mutashābihāt* is inconsistent with examination or test, and those who follow the *mutashābihāt* do not intend to torture and torment others. It does not mean to heat or burn either. Rather, they are sedition-mongers because under the pretext of the allegorical verses, they intend to create agitation or doubt in the minds of people and misguide them.

The Qur'anic stance vis-à-vis sedition [fitnah] in religion

"Sedition in religion" in the above sense can be considered as masked confrontation by the elements of deception and trickery. This activity is undertaken with the aim of uprooting the essence of religion under the garb of ostentatious faith. Through hypocrisy [*nifāq*], sedition-mongers keep their satanic ideas secret so that it becomes difficult for the common people to detect their anti-religious motives. For this reason, the Qur'an has considered it the gravest sin and informed people of the greatest of dangers in this world and the hereafter, urging them to rise up and exert all their efforts to defend their religion.

The enemies usually approach confronting Islam and the Muslims in two ways. The Qur'an also offers guidance in dealing with the enemies' conspiracies.

1. Armed sedition

One of the enemies' conventional ways of confronting Islam and the Muslims is physical combat or open war. By military invasion of Muslim countries, killing of Muslims and plundering their resources, they strive to achieve their objectives. In this way, they kill a number of Muslims and destroy Muslim countries but they never attain their goals. By getting killed for the sake of religion, not only do Muslims not suffer any loss but their belief becomes stronger and more formidable. In religious culture, the goal of life in this world is the perfection of man and the attainment of divine

1 *Sūrah al-Anbiyā'* 21:35.

2 *Sūrah Āl 'Imrān* 3:7.

proximity through belief, worship and servitude to God, its highest degree being martyrdom in the way of God.

Meanwhile, the stance of the Qur'an against this strategy of the enemies is as follows:

﴿ وَقَاتِلُوهُمْ حَتَّى لاَ تَكُونَ فِتْنَةٌ وَيَكُونَ الدِّينُ كُلُّهُ لِلّه ﴾

> *"Fight them until faithlessness*[1] *is no more, and religion becomes exclusively for Allah."*[2]

In this fighting, the slogan of the Muslims is as follows:

﴿ قُلْ هَلْ تَرَبَّصُونَ بِنَا إِلاَّ إِحْدَى الْحُسْنَيَيْنِ وَنَحْنُ نَتَرَبَّصُ بِكُمْ أَن يُصِيبَكُمُ اللّهُ بِعَذَابٍ مِّنْ عِندِهِ أَوْ بِأَيْدِينَا فَتَرَبَّصُواْ إِنَّا مَعَكُم مُّتَرَبِّصُونَ ﴾

> *"Say, 'Do you await anything to befall us except one of the two excellences? But we await that Allah shall visit on you a punishment, from Him, or by our hands. So wait! We too are waiting along with you.'"*[3]

2. Cultural sedition

The second main approach of the enemies in confronting Islam and the Muslims consists of cultural activities which instill doubt in the hearts of the Muslims. The approach, means and tools, methods and consequences used in this type of conflict are different from a military attack. In a military attack the enemy comes to the front with the most advanced weapons to physically kill the Muslims and plunder their resources, in the cultural attack pen and speech are used to mislead and corrupt the minds of Muslims. In a military attack the enemy confronts the Muslim combatants in the harshest way possible, in the cultural onslaught the enemy pretends to be full of "sympathy and concern". In a military attack the Muslims can see the enemy, while in the cultural onslaught identifying the enemy is not an easy task. In a military attack the enemy intends to eliminate physical bodies by the use of mines and advanced weapons, in the cultural onslaught he intends to win hearts and minds towards his interests by brainwashing them.

In a military attack the enemy has the capability to send off only a specific number of Muslim combatants from this base materialistic world, in the cultural onslaught the devils lie in ambush to allure the innocent youth—the

---

1 Or 'polytheism.' Cf. *Sūrah al-Baqarah* 2:193. [Qur'an Trans.]

2 *Sūrah al-Anfāl* 8:39.

3 *Sūrah al-Tawbah* (or, *Barā'ah*) 9:52.

greatest asset of a Muslim nation that does not have sufficient knowledge of the religious sciences and precepts—and drown it in irreligiousness. It is true that the enemies will not derive advantage from this coquetry against religion and the Muslim nation, because our educated Muslim youth, who honorably and victoriously emerged from the armed struggle and invasion, are vigilant enough to detect the enemy's transfer from the military front to the cultural front. Yet, because of the gravity of the danger and the irreparability of the consequences of defeat on the cultural front, the Holy Qur'an, while warning the Muslims, urges them to stand firmly against the enemies of God and religion.

The warning of the Qur'an against cultural sedition

Since the felicity of the Muslims in this world and the hereafter will be jeopardized in case of negligence, the Qur'an warns the Muslims against cultural sedition, and regards it as more serious than a military assault.

The Holy Qur'an says:

﴿ وَاقْتُلُوهُمْ حَيْثُ ثَقِفْتُمُوهُمْ وَأَخْرِجُوهُم مِّنْ حَيْثُ أَخْرَجُوكُمْ وَالْفِتْنَةُ أَشَدُّ مِنَ الْقَتْلِ ﴾

"And kill them wherever you confront them and expel them from where they expelled you, for faithlessness[1] is graver than killing."[2]

Of course, we are aware that the opponents of the Qur'an during its revelation and the advent of Islam, mostly participated in military aggression to extinguish Islam and the Muslims. Yet, the Qur'an gives more emphasis to the menace of cultural and religious sedition than military aggression. The Qur'an states:

﴿ وَالْفِتْنَةُ أَكْبَرُ مِنَ الْقَتْلِ ﴾

"And faithlessness is graver than killing."[3]

That is, polytheism is more dangerous than military aggression and killing, and the sin of its commission is graver than that of killing Muslims.

Polytheism [shirk] under a new garb

Polytheism [*shirk*] has existed alongside monotheism [*tawḥīd*] throughout the history of mankind. Those who refused to submit to the Creator of the

1 Or 'polytheism'. [Qur'an Trans.]

2 *Sūrah al-Baqarah* 2:190-191.

3 *Sūrah al-Baqarah* 2:217.

universe have been in pursuit of satisfying their carnal desires and constantly obstructed the monotheists in various ways.

The proponents of polytheism cleverly adopted the lifestyle of people of the time and chose appropriate methods to achieve their objectives. As such, since polytheism manifested itself in the form of idol-worship during the early period of Islam, the chiefs of polytheism promoted the worship of idols made of stone and wood, and prevented people from inclining to the worship of One God. The reason behind this attitude was that with the dominance of the monotheistic culture, there would have been no room for them to satisfy their carnal desires.

Today, polytheism in its modern form is promoted under the guise of "scientific theories" in different gatherings and circles. If during the early period of Islam 360 idols or so were worshipped and promoted by materialists to stupefy the minds of people, today the exponents of polytheism try to build as many idols as the people, dissuade them from thinking of God, the Exalted, and draw their attention to satanic insinuations and superstitions.

It is clear that the notion of "straight paths" or "different interpretations of religion" belongs to this category, since it means that any person can take whatever he understands regarding God and religion from the religious texts as the basis of his belief and action because that is the truth and reality.

Therefore, everyone can have his own private or personal deities and religions. It is evident that this notion is diametrically opposed to the spirit of monotheism which is embodied in the formula of faith *"There is no god but Allah"* [*Lā ilāha ill*allāh].

Since the most sensitive subject in the life of man is his belief, on which his felicity in this world and the hereafter depends, it is worthwhile for him to reexamine his beliefs and ideas on the basis of the Qur'an and the teachings of the *Ahl al-Bayt* (*'a*), and rationally or logically assess them without being led astray by his whims and caprice, for it is only in this way that he can free himself from the snares of Satan and the abyss of deviation. Of course, to purify one's self and overcome one's carnal desires is extremely difficult, and it is not without purpose that the Apostle (*ṣ*) has considered it "greater *jihād*" [*jihād al-akbar*]. It is especially true if the enemies of monotheism and Islam are willing to grant him international fame in order to achieve their political and colonial agendas of confronting Islam. It is true that in such a situation, for man to embark on *jihād al-akbar*, and disregard the pledges and promises of the enemies of Islam is an astounding and amazing accomplishment, but it is not impossible. In history, many individuals came to their senses at the last moment, freed themselves from their carnal desires and the trap of the devils from among the jinn and humans, saved themselves from impending perdition, and returned to the fold of monotheism.

The prediction of the Qur'an about the emergence of sedition in religion

The Holy Qur'an has shown the Muslims the ways to attain perfection and bliss. Like a luminous torch that will never be extinguished, it has made the straight path of guidance clear to the seekers of truth. The Apostle (*ṣ*) also washed the dust and filth of polytheism off the face of humanity, implanted the seed of hope and deliverance in the hearts of those who were thirsting for truth and made it fruitful, and founded a government based upon monotheism. Meanwhile, many became Muslims out of expediency and their faith was not beyond oral declaration. True belief in God did not enter their hearts. Naturally, such individuals gave preference to their carnal desires over the will of God and the orders of the Apostle (*ṣ*). During the lifetime of the Apostle (*ṣ*), the secret enemies of Islam and the Apostle (*ṣ*) did not consider it expedient to openly express their hostility and divulge their plot to change the direction of the divine government, oppose the infallible Imāms (*'a*) and deprive the people of their divinely guided leadership. These devils and worldly people waited for the passing away of the Apostle (*ṣ*) to implement their sinister schemes.

Predicting this conspiracy, the Holy Qur'an gives this warning:

﴿ أَحَسِبَ النَّاسُ أَن يُتْرَكُوا أَن يَقُولُوا آمَنَّا وَهُمْ لا يُفْتَنُونَ ﴾

"Do the people suppose that they will be let off because they say, 'We have faith,' and they will not be tested?"[1]

The prediction of *fitnah* after his demise by the Apostle (*ṣ*)

One day, Ḥaḍrat 'Alī (*'a*) was talking about the Qur'an, inviting the people to firmly cling to the divine stronghold [*ḥabl'ul-matīn*] and follow its instructions, and giving glad tidings of felicity in paradise to the faithful, and warning the hypocrites and seditionists of chastisement in hell. A man stood up and asked about sedition and requested Imām 'Alī (*ṣ*) to quote a saying of the Apostle (*ṣ*) in this regard. In reply, the Imām (*'a*) recalled the moment of revelation of the verse, *"Do the people suppose that they will be let off because they say, 'We have faith,' and they will not be tested?"* and how the Apostle (*ṣ*) informed the people of the occurrence of *fitnah* in religion a great test. He said he understood that this *fitnah* would occur after

1 *Sūrah al-'Ankabūt* 29:2.

the demise of the Apostle (ṣ), and asked the Apostle (ṣ) about the nature of *fitnah* in religion that would take place as mentioned by God, the Exalted. The Apostle (ṣ) said: 'After me my *ummah* will experience *fitnah*.' He (ṣ) then mentioned the types of sedition (*fitnah*) that would be carried out by the materialists, emphasizing three types:

يَا عَلِيٌّ إِنَّ الْقَوْمَ سَيُفْتَنُوْنَ بِأَمْوَالِهِمْ وَيَمُنُّوْنَ بِدِيْنِهِمْ عَلَى رَبِّهِمْ وَيَتَمَنَّوْنَ رَحْمَتَهُ وَيَأْمَنُوْنَ سَطْوَتَهُ يَسْتَحِلُّوْنَ حَرَامَهُ بِالشُّبَهَاتِ الْكَاذِبَةِ وَالأَهْوَاءِ السَّاهِيَةِ، فَيَسْتَحِلُّوْنَ الْخَمْرَ بِالنَّبِيْذِ وَالسُّحْتَ بِالْهَدِيَّةِ وَالرِّبَا بِالْبَيْعِ

O 'Alī! Surely the people will be tested with their wealth. They will count as a favor to their Lord their acceptance of the religion and expect His mercy and immunity from punishment. They will make lawful what He prohibited through unjustifiable misgivings and carnal desires. So they will equate wine with fruit syrup, bribery with gift, and usury [*ribā*] with trade."

1. Financial fitnah

The first type the Apostle (ṣ) mentioned was *fitnah* in matters of wealth. Those who are familiar with Islamic jurisprudence [*fiqh*] know that a large number of the practical laws of Islam deal with wealth, business, trade, and economic affairs. In Islam, individual rights have been given the best possible attention. The rules and regulations in commercial, business and trade transactions have been enacted based on the real interests of man's social life. By observing them, people can have felicity in this world and the hereafter. Economic relations in society are mostly undertaken in the form of trade or buying and selling, and the edifice of social life is founded on social transactions, cooperation and helping one another in solving problems. On account of the profiteering instinct of man, usurious transactions—the worst and most abhorrent type of transaction according to Islam—have been widespread among people which the Qur'an has sternly prohibited the people from undertaking. The tone of the Qur'anic prohibition of this practice is so admonishing that it regards it as tantamount to waging war against God:

﴿ فَإِن لَّمْ تَفْعَلُوا فَأْذَنُوا بِحَرْبٍ مِنَ اللّهِ ﴾

"And if you do not [desist from practicing usury], then be informed of a war from Allah."[1]

1 *Sūrah al-Baqarah* 2:279.

The Apostle (ṣ) said: "After me the people will be afflicted with a *fitnah* in their wealth and economic relations, ignore the explicit decrees of the Qur'an on the prohibition of usury, and practice usury under the pretext of trade and business based on false justifications."

2. Ideological fitnah

It is God, the Exalted, who has created the universe and granted us the blessing of existence. He has completed His favor upon us human beings by sending His best servants along with heavenly scriptures for us to attain perfection and bliss. Gratitude for the blessing of guidance can be expressed only by acknowledgment of servitude to God which is the highest conceivable station of man.

It is abominable, detestable and loathsome to find ignorant man feel he is doing God a favor by accepting His guidance and ordinances, and not to know that God actually deserves our gratitude, for it is He who has guided us to the religion of truth.

Addressing the Apostle (ṣ), the Holy Qur'an states:

﴿ يَمُنُّونَ عَلَيْكَ أَنْ أَسْلَمُوا قُل لَّا تَمُنُّوا عَلَيَّ إِسْلَامَكُم بَلِ اللَّهُ يَمُنُّ عَلَيْكُمْ أَنْ هَدَاكُمْ لِلْإِيمَانِ ﴾

"They count it as a favor to you that they have embraced Islam. Say, 'Do not count it as a favor to me your embracing Islam. Rather it is Allah who has done you a favor in that He has guided you to faith.'"[1]

Therefore, from the religious perspective, the criterion is servitude and submission to God, and not self-centeredness and the feeling of arrogance vis-à-vis God. The Apostle (ṣ) presents self-centeredness and the feeling of arrogance in lieu of the spirit of servitude and submission to God as one of the manifestations of *fitnah* in religion. The Prophet (ṣ) said: "After me, one of the manifestations of *fitnah* in religion is that instead of being grateful to God for the blessing of religion and divine guidance, people will feel God should be indebted to them for their acceptance of His religion and expect His reward and mercy as a matter of right! Similarly, for embracing Islam they will arrogantly think they should not deserve any punishment. It is true that God, the Exalted, does not punish His servant for no reason, but the Apostle (ṣ) regards having such a feeling as *fitnah* in religion, for those who have this feeling—whenever observance of a religious ordinance is inconsistent with their carnal desires—would easily deceive themselves and others through baseless justifications. As such, to have a sense of arrogance

1 *Sūrah al-Ḥujurāt* 49:17.

vis-à-vis God is repugnant to the truth of religion and the spirit of Islam, which is total submission to the Will of God.

3. False justifications as the most dangerous fitnah

The most dangerous *fitnah* which worried the Apostle (*ṣ*) and which he warned the people by mentioning it to Ḥaḍrat 'Alī (*'a*) is the *fitnah* or conspiracy of distortion [*taḥrīf*] in religion and passing a verdict on what God has prohibited. It is true that non-observance of religious laws [*sharī'ah*] and a sense of arrogance vis-à-vis Almighty God is indeed a cardinal sin, but what is more serious is to fabricate false justifications for anti-religious activities and give a religious color to carnal desires.

In this case, Satan rushes to the rescue of materialistic Muslims and assists them by distorting religious laws.

The Apostle (*ṣ*) said that in order to serve their carnal desires, the *fitnah*-mongers resort to doubts, false justifications and futile arguments to declare lawful what God has prohibited and make a mockery of His religion.

What is worth mentioning is that the Apostle (*ṣ*) specially mentioned the persistence of the *fitnah*s that would continue to exist until the advent of Ḥaḍrat Ṣāḥib al-Amr,[1] the Imām of the Time (*'a*). What the Apostle (*ṣ*) mentioned as examples of *fitnah*s such as wine being regarded as lawful under the pretext that it is the same lawful fruit syrup or juice, or bribery as synonymous with giving gifts, or usury as identical with trade are only a few of the *fitnah*s in religion, and they are not confined to these examples.

Nowadays, there are Muslims who do not consider themselves outside the fold of Islam, but in reality they do not faithfully accept the divine laws. Those who have social positions acquire a self-defeating attitude due to the influence of Western culture and become alien to their religious identity. On the other hand, their knowledge of religious sciences is not sufficient. Meanwhile, notwithstanding their incompetence in expressing views on specialized religious issues, they dare to give verdicts and are sometimes influenced by satanic insinuations and encouraged by the enemies of religion. Consciously or unconsciously, their conversation means nothing but the denial of religion and going outside the fold of Islam. For example, if a person asserts that the laws of Islam are applicable only to the people of that period, and that in the 21st century, the Qur'an and the laws of Islam are not capable of administering society, and its laws and ordinances must be changed according to the demands and discretion of the people, or that

---

1 *Ṣāḥib al-Amr* [The Owner/Master of the Affair]: one of the titles of Imām al-Mahdī (*'a*). [Trans.]

the people of the 21st century need a prophet who is appropriate for the time, such assertions can be considered not only a denial of religion but the claimants' incorrect understanding of religion and its laws. Those who make such assertions are supposed to pay attention to the implication, corollaries and repercussions of their assertions. Perhaps they would avoid saying something that could be considered seditious in religion and save themselves from the snare of Satan and the enemies of Islam and the Qur'an.

Obscuring the atmosphere with the aim of misleading public opinion

The modus operandi of the enemies of religion and the Qur'an in creating *fitnah* and military aggression is totally different from their way of undertaking cultural onslaught and sedition. Opposed to military aggression, in the cultural *fitnah* they never openly show themselves denying religion and opposing the religious culture of the people, or openly express their true beliefs. What exists in our society as cultural *fitnah* currently is that the enemies of the Qur'an and religious culture obscure the cultural atmosphere in such a manner that the people, especially the educated youth, lose the power of identifying truth from falsehood and unconsciously fall into the trap of their false notions and deviant beliefs. Naturally, if the educated class of a country is afflicted with intellectual deviation, the door for misguidance and deviation of the public will also be opened, because

إذَا فَسَدَ الْعَالِمُ فَسَدَ الْعَالَمُ.

"If the scholar ['ālim] is corrupt, the world ['ālam] is corrupted."[1]

Therefore, cultural *fitnah* as warned by the Apostle (ṣ) is one of the most dangerous things that threaten people's felicity in this world and the hereafter.

It is clear that in dealing with such threats, the Islamic state must be so forceful in stating the truths of religion and propagating the culture and teachings of the Qur'an, and supervise the educational system from pre-school to university and all cultural centers that the malevolent enemies of Islam cannot mislead others by means of obscuring the cultural atmosphere.

On the other hand, the most fundamental duty of the religious scholars is to enlighten the people, especially the youth, who do not have sufficient knowledge of religious teachings and Qur'anic sciences, and combat cultural *fitnah*. The religious scholars are obliged to inform the people, especially the young generation, of the cultural threats and conspiracy of the

1 *Ghurar al-Ḥikam*, vol. 7, p. 269. [Trans.]

enemies of religion and keep them away from the snares of Satan. Religious people can assist committed religious scholars in accomplishing their great mission of guiding society.

As stated at the beginning of the book, in this part we shall mention the motives of the opponents of religious culture as recorded in *Nahj al-Balāghah* by Imām 'Alī (*'a*). We shall first identify these elements and then mention the motives of these individuals in opposing religious culture and the teachings of the Qur'an.

Distorters of religious teachings according to 'Alī ('a)

Imām 'Alī (*'a*) named those who distort the truths of religion and corrupt the religious culture of the people as "pseudo-learned ignoramuses". The Imām (*'a*) said:

وَآخَرُ قَدْ تَسَمَّى عَالِماً وَلَيْسَ بِهِ.

> "While the other (kind of) man is he who calls himself learned but he is not so."[1]

Opposing the upright followers of the Qur'an are a group of people who are sometimes considered scholars though in reality they are not so. By the use of fictitious and false titles, they mislead the people. They present their arguments as an interpretation of religion and the Qur'an. About them, Ḥaḍrat 'Alī ('a) said:

فَاقْتَبَسَ جَهَائِلَ مِنْ جُهَّالٍ.

> "He has gleaned ignorance from the ignorant."[2]

In other words what they assert as academic subjects and interpretations of religion and intend to impose religious beliefs under the pretext of different interpretations of religion, are elements of ignorance they have acquired from fellow ignoramuses. Perhaps, you may wonder how an ignorant could learn something from another ignorant! What does it mean by "an ignorant learning from another ignorant"?! In order to become aware of the wonders of the words of Imām 'Alī (*'a*) and become more informed of our responsibility to enlighten people of such deviators from truth, we shall cite an example of pseudo-learned ignoramuses learning from fellow ignoramuses through what they call "scientific methods".

---

1 *Nahj al-Balāghah*, Sermon 86.

2 *Ibid.*

In the West today it is believed that acquisition of knowledge is impossible for man and he must be skeptical of everything and have no certainty in any subject. The proponents of this idea believe that for a person to say that he is certain of the certain subject is a sign of ignorance and folly, for it is impossible to have knowledge of anything. Being proud of this doubt and ignorance, they argue that the sign of knowledge, learning and intelligence is for man to be skeptical of any knowledge and certainty in any subject whether religious or non-religious. Such weak arguments have been advanced for the past one hundred years or so among the Europeans. Prior to it, it had also been the intellectual basis of the skeptics. In our society today, there are those who intend to weaken the religious convictions of the people by casting doubt upon their religious beliefs under the pretext that we cannot have certain knowledge in any field, and, thereby, realize their goals and satisfy their carnal desires. Interestingly enough, they advance these contentions under the guise of "academic subjects" and expect our wary and sagacious people to accept them hook, line and sinker.

Ḥaḍrat 'Alī (*'a*) pointed to the existence of such wicked individuals throughout history and said:

فَاقْتَبَسَ جَهَائِلَ مِنْ جُهَّال وَأَضَالِيلَ مِنْ ضُلاَّل.

> "He has gleaned ignorance from the ignorant and misguidance from the misguided."[1]

They learn ridiculous subjects from a group of ignorant and misguided persons and discuss them as "scientific facts". An example of their "scientific facts" is that one must doubt everything and not have certainty in anything! Concerning religious affairs, they say whatever a person understands is the truth! It is because in essence truth and falsehood do not exist! There is no criterion for truth and falsehood except the personal understanding of every person.

Imām 'Alī (*'a*) also said:

وَنَصَبَ لِلنَّاسِ أَشْرَاكاً مِنْ حبالِ غُرُور، وَقَوْلِ زُور.

> "He has set for the people a trap (made) of the ropes of deceit and untrue speech."[2]

The Imām (*'a*) continued:

---

1 *Ibid.*

2 *Ibid.*

قَدْ حَمَلَ الْكِتَابَ عَلَى آرَائِهِ.

"He takes the Book (Qur'an) according to his own views and right after his passions."[1]

Then, the Imām (*'a*) turned his attention to the propaganda styles of these people and said:

وَعَطَفَ الْحَقَّ عَلى أَهْوَائِهِ، يُؤْمِنُ مِنَ الْعَظَائِمِ، وَيُهَوِّنُ كَبِيرَ الْجَرَائِمِ.

"He makes people feel safe from big sins and treats serious crimes lightly."[2]

That is, in a bid to draw the attention of people, they make them feel safe from the consequences of their major sins, present major sins as trivial, and thus encourage them to commit crimes and offenses. They actually try to weaken religious convictions and piety.

The Imām (*'a*) also said:

يَقُولُ: أَقِفُ عِنْدَ الشُّبُهَاتِ، وَفِيهَا وَقَعَ، وَيَقُولُ: أَعْتَزِلُ الْبِدَعَ، وَبَيْنَهَا اضْطَجَعَ. فَالصُّورَةُ صُورَةُ إِنْسَانٍ، وَالْقَلْبُ قَلْبُ حَيَوَانٍ، لاَ يَعْرِفُ بَابَ الْهُدَى فَيَتَّبِعَهُ، وَلاَ بَابَ الْعَمَى فَيَصُدَّ عَنْهُ، فَذلِكَ مَيِّتُ الأَحْيَاءِ!

"He says that he is waiting for (clarification of) doubts but he remains plunged therein, and that he keeps aloof from innovations but actually he is immersed in them. His shape is that of a man, but his heart is that of a beast. He does not know the door of guidance to follow or the door of misguidance to keep aloof from. Such people are living dead bodies."[3]

Then, Imām 'Alī (*'a*) addressed the people and said:

(فَأَيْنَ تَذْهَبُونَ)؟ و (أَنَّى تُؤْفَكُونَ)! وَالأَعْلاَمُ قَائِمَةٌ، وَالآيَاتُ وَاضِحَةٌ، وَالْمَنَارُ مَنْصُوبَةٌ، فَأَيْنَ يُتَاهُ بِكُمْ؟ بَلْ كَيْفَ تَعْمَهُونَ وَبَيْنَكُمْ عِتْرَةُ نَبِيِّكُمْ؟ وَهُمْ أَزِمَّةُ الْحَقِّ، وَأَلْسِنَةُ الصِّدْقِ! فَأَنْزِلُوهُمْ بِأَحْسَنِ مَنَازِلِ الْقُرْآنِ، وَرِدُوهُمْ وُرُودَ الْهِيمِ الْعِطَاشِ.

""'So where are you going?"[4] "Then where do you stray?"[5] The signs (of guidance) are standing, indications (of virtue) are clear,

---

1 *Ibid.*

2 *Ibid.*

3 *Ibid.*

4 *Sūrah al-Takwīr* 81:26.

5 *Sūrah al-An'ām* 6:95; *Sūrah Yūnus* 10:34; *Sūrah Fātir* 35:3; *Sūrah al-Ghāfir* (or *al-Mu'min*) 40:62.

> and the minarets (of light) have been fixed. Where are you being taken astray and how are you groping while you have among you the descendants of the Prophet? They are the reins of Right, signs of Faith and tongues of truth. Accord to them the same good position as you accord to the Qur'an, and come to them (for quenching the thirst of guidance) as thirsty camels approach the water spring."[1]

In a tone harsher than that of Hadrat 'Alī (*'a*), the Holy Qur'an describes these pseudo-learned ignoramuses and warns the people of their deception:

﴿ وَكَذَلِكَ جَعَلْنَا لِكُلِّ نبِيٍّ عَدُوًّا شَيَاطِينَ الإِنسِ وَالْجِنِّ يُوحِي بَعْضُهُمْ إِلَى بَعْضٍ زُخْرُفَ الْقَوْلِ غُرُورًا وَلَوْ شَاء رَبُّكَ مَا فَعَلُوهُ فَذَرْهُمْ وَمَا يَفْتَرُونَ ﴾

> *"That is how for every prophet We appointed as enemies the devils from among humans and jinn, who inspired each other with flashy words, deceptively. Had your Lord wished, they would not have done it. So leave them with what they fabricate."*[2]

The enemies of the prophets (*'a*) and the opponents of divine guidance are outwardly human but because all their activities are directed towards misguiding others, instilling doubts, weakening religious beliefs, and opposing divine guidance, the Qur'an describes them as devils in human form and warns people from following them.

Pseudo-Muslim materialists' treatment of the Qur'an

Those whose faith is not strong will not be pleased with religion, and always be inclined to interpret and justify religious laws and values according to their whims and carnal desires. If only their interpretation of religion and the Qur'an according to their carnal desires were permitted, it would be very pleasant for this group for then they could satisfy their carnal desires and keep enjoying the privileges of being Muslims in an Islamic society. Similarly, it is natural that those who are not attached to the religious values and divine laws welcome such interpretations of religion and the Qur'an. They follow those who interpret and justify religion, the Qur'an and religious values according to their carnal desires, take them as their models and express gratitude. It is equally natural that such individuals are not in terms with religious scholars who interpret and expound the Qur'an and its laws as they are, without considering the pleasure and preference of individuals and people.

---

1 *Nahj al-Balāghah*, Sermon 86.

2 *Sūrah al-An'ām* 6:112.

It is indeed a pity that today we can witness those who, under the pretext of "different interpretations of religious texts," intend to give a religious color to their own carnal desires and yearnings and make a mockery of the religion of God and the Holy Qur'an.

By predicting the condition of society, Hadrat 'Alī (*'a*) complained of the alienation of the Qur'an during his time as well as the end of time, saying:

إِلَى اللهِ أَشْكُومِن مَعشَرٍ يَعِيشُونَ جُهَّالاً، وَيَمُوتُونَ ضُلَّالاً، لَيْسَ فِيهِمْ سِلْعَةٌ أَبْوَرُ مِنَ الكِتَابِ إِذَا تُلِيَ حَقَّ تِلاوَتِهِ، وَلاَ سِلْعَةٌ أَنْفَقُ بَيْعاً وَلاَ أَغْلَى ثَمَناً مِنَ الكِتَابِ إِذَا حُرِّفَ عَنْ مَوَاضِعِهِ!

"I complain to Allah about persons who live ignorant and die misguided. For them nothing is more worthless than the Qur'an if it is recited as it should be recited, nor anything more valuable than the Qur'an if its verses are removed from their places."[1]

Similarly, regarding the status of the Qur'an and religious teachings during the end of time, Imām 'Alī (*'a*) thus said:

وَإِنَّهُ سَيَأْتِي عَلَيْكُمْ مِنْ بَعْدِي زَمَانٌ لَيْسَ فِيهِ شَيْءٌ أَخْفَى مِنَ الْحَقِّ، وَلاَ أَظْهَرَ مِنَ الْبَاطِلِ، وَلاَ أَكْثَرَ مِنَ الْكَذِبِ عَلَى اللهِ وَرَسُولِهِ، وَلَيْسَ عِنْدَ أَهْلِ ذلِكَ الزَّمَانِ سِلْعَةٌ أَبْوَرَ مِنَ الْكِتَابِ إِذَا تُلِيَ حَقَّ تِلاوَتِهِ، وَلاَ أَنْفَقَ مِنْهُ إِذَا حُرِّفَ عَنْ مَوَاضِعِهِ، وَلاَ فِي الْبِلاَدِ شَيْءٌ أَنْكَرَ مِنَ الْمَعْرُوفِ، وَلاَ أَعْرَفَ مِنَ الْمُنكَرِ! فَقَدْ نَبَذَ الْكِتَابَ حَمَلَتُهُ، وَتَنَاسَاهُ حَفَظَتُهُ، فَالْكِتَابُ يَوْمَئِذٍ وَأَهْلُهُ مَنْفِيَّانِ طَرِيدَانِ، وَصَاحِبَانِ مُصْطَحِبَانِ فِي طَرِيقٍ وَاحِدٍ لاَ يُؤْوِيهِمَا مُؤْوٍ، فَالْكِتَابُ وَأَهْلُهُ فِي ذلِكَ الزَّمَانِ فِي النَّاسِ وَلَيْسَا فِيهِمْ، وَمَعَهُمْ وَلَيْسَا مَعَهُمْ! لاِنَّ الضَّلاَلَةَ لاَ تُوَافِقُ الْهُدَى، وَإِنِ اجْتَمَعَا، فَاجْتَمَعَ الْقَوْمُ عَلَى الْفُرْقَةِ، وَافْتَرَقُوا عَنِ الْجَمَاعَةِ، كَأَنَّهُمْ أَئِمَّةُ الْكِتَابِ وَلَيْسَ الْكِتَابُ إِمَامَهُمْ.

"Certainly, a time will come upon you after me when nothing will be more concealed than rightfulness, nothing more apparent than wrongfulness and nothing more current than untruth against Allah and His Prophet. For the people of this period nothing will be more valueless than the Qur'an being recited as it ought to be recited, nor anything more valuable than the Qur'an being misplaced from its position. And in the towns nothing will be more hated than virtue, nor anything more acceptable than vice. The holders of the Book will throw it away and its memorizers forget it. In these days the Qur'an and its people will be exiled and expelled. They will be companions keeping together on one path, but no one will offer them asylum. Consequently at this time the Qur'an and its people

1 *Ibid.*, Sermon 17.

> will be among the people but not among them, will be with them but not with them, because misguidance cannot accord with guidance even though they may be together. The people will have united on division and will therefore be cut away from the community, as though they were the leaders of the Qur'an and not the Qur'an their leader."[1]

The Commander of the Faithful (*'a*) clearly predicted that after him a time will come when nothing will be more concealed than the truth and nothing more apparent than falsehood. Lies and calumny against God and His Apostle (*ṣ*) will frequently be done by the pseudo-learned ignoramuses and materialistic hypocrite s in order to attain their goals.

Imām 'Alī's (*'a*) warning to the people

The point worth noting and being warned about is that it portrays and describes the spiritual and cultural state of the masses in the future. It is true that the Qur'anic verses and statements of Hadrat 'Alī (*'a*) discussed and examined in this book are addressed to the people, but most of them are addressed to the elite of society and those who can exert influence on the culture of society. In this sermon, Imām 'Alī (*'a*) explicitly predicts the spiritual state and religious culture of the people in the future and warns them of the affliction of such a culture and negligence of truth. After describing the dominant spirit of a section of the elite of society who, in order to advance their worldly objectives and desires, would mostly attribute lies and calumnies to God and the Apostle (*ṣ*), interpret the Qur'an and religion according to their personal opinions, and misguide the people, the Imām (*'a*) predicted the dominant culture of the masses in this manner:

"The people at that time would also be such that if the Book of Allah (Qur'an) were correctly and rightfully interpreted and explained, it would become one of the most valueless things for them and if it were interpreted according to their carnal desires, it would become the most valuable and lovable of things for them. At that time, the religious or divine values will be the most abominable things for the people while the anti-religious values will be the most cherished things for them."

It is known to those who are informed that today the enemies of the Qur'an and the arrogant powers want such a culture to prevail in our society. In line with the cultural onslaught conspiracy, by attacking the religious sanctities and launching anti-religious propaganda, they strive for such conditions as predicted by the Commander of the Faithful (*'a*).

---

1 *Ibid.*, Sermon 147.

In continuation, Imām 'Alī (*'a*) said: "At that time, no action will be seen from those who are knowledgeable of the Word of God except indifference, and from the protectors of the Qur'an whose duty is to guard the religious values nothing but complacency and negligence in the performance of duty. At that time, the Qur'an and its true followers and the religious scholars will be among the people but in reality separate from them and the people will be equally away from them. It is because the people will isolate them and not follow them. They will live among the people but the hearts of the people will not be with them because the people will tread the path of misguidance, which cannot be reconciled with the way of the Qur'an, the path of guidance.

At the end of the sermon, Imām 'Alī (*'a*) thus said: "The people will have united on division and will therefore have cut away from the Islamic community, as though they were the leaders of the Qur'an and not the Qur'an their leader." That is, the people at that time will be united on discord and dissension. It is as if they will agree on not to concur with the Qur'an and its true interpreters, to follow the pseudo-learned ignoramuses as though they were the leaders of the Qur'an and will interpret and justify the Qur'an according to their carnal desires, and to separate and keep aloof from the true Muslims, religious scholars and authentic interpreters of the Qur'an. Instead of taking the Qur'an as their guide and model in their thinking and action, they will overtake the Qur'an, refuse to acknowledge its leadership and guidance and interpret the Qur'an and religion according to their opinion."

Now, the enemies of religion and the Qur'an have tried their best to remove the religious identity of the Muslim nation and deprive them of their independence, freedom and honor by means of weakening their religious beliefs. Considering the importance and sensitivity of the situation, it is expedient for the Muslim nation, especially the religious scholars, to realize the threat, be vigilant and never be complacent concerning their situation vis-à-vis the threat posed by the enemies of Islam and the Qur'an.

Meanwhile, as mentioned earlier, in a bid to achieve their imperialist agenda, the enemies of Islam and global *kufr* do not openly express their enmity to Islam and the Muslim *ummah* in confronting the religious culture of the people. They usually utilize those Muslim elements living in the Islamic society who, on one hand, have social and cultural positions and, on the other hand, have somehow religious credentials. Knowingly or unknowingly, they who are tools in the hands of foreign agents pave the ground for the misguidance of people by distorting religious teachings. These individuals have been condemned and reproached in many verses of the Holy Qur'an and traditions of the infallible Imāms (*'a*) and the people have been warned about them.

The motive of pseudo-learned ignoramuses in distorting religious teachings according to 'Alī (*'a*)

As I have said earlier, the Holy Qur'an labeled the activity of such people as *fitnah* and those who intend to distort the Qur'an and the religious truths and teachings are *fitnah*-mongers who come to the rescue of Satan in misguiding the people. Now, this question may possibly be asked: Why in spite of knowing the truth and being aware of the groundlessness of the superstitions they have acquired, are they determined to justify their misguidance of people? In other words: What is the psychological problem of those who intend to distort religious teachings and misguide people? In reality, what is the origin of *fitnah* in religion which is actualized in the form of distortion of religious teachings?

In reply to this question, Hadrat 'Alī (*'a*) said:

إِنَّمَا بَدْءُ وُقُوعِ الْفِتَنِ أَهْوَاءٌ تُتَّبَعُ، وَأَحْكَامٌ تُبْتَدَعُ.

> "The basis of the occurrence of evils consists of those desires which are acted upon and the orders that are innovated."[1]

The seditions [*fitan*] in religion emanate from carnal desires, worldly yearnings and cravings. Those who misguide the people by means of distorting the religious teachings have lost their spirit of surrender and submission to God, the Exalted, as a result of satanic insinuations and temptations.

The spirit of servitude and submission to God demands that man be faithful to Islamic laws and religious values in words and deeds, because many religious ordinances might not be consistent with his carnal desires, and he may not be willing to sincerely accept and abide by them. In such cases, human beings are always in a state of dilemma and have no option but to choose the will of God and Islamic law and oppose their carnal desires, or prefer their carnal desires and whims over the will of God. In this great test, most people are overcome by their carnal desires, and they prefer their personal desires over the will of God and religious values. Some of them have the courage to say: "We are bound by the religious beliefs and values. We will not distort and oppose religious values." This kind of attitude towards religion cannot be considered *fitnah* in religion because no one has been misguided by deception.

1 *Nahj al-Balāghah*, Sermon 50.

The lack of the spirit of submission and servitude to God and His decrees can be a source of *fitnah* when those who lack this spirit intend through false justifications to interpret religion according to their carnal desires.

If such individuals enjoy a social status on account of which some people listen to them, they are more than any other the object of Satan's temptation, because they have desires which have been prohibited by religion, and it is difficult for them to dispense with them on account of the weakness of their spirit of servitude to God. Meanwhile, they have the power by the use of which they can present the truth in their favor. Satan exploits this golden opportunity, and draws and incites them to *fitnah* and the distortion of religion. Satan kindles the fire of satisfying these desires in their hearts. He also instills this doubt in their minds: What is the proof that what the religious scholars have declared as religious obligations and values are exactly what God or religion wants from us?

Since such individuals observe that with the existence of the Qur'an, the sayings of the *'ulamā'*, and the teachings of the *Ahl al-Bayt* (*'a*), they cannot fully satisfy their carnal desires, whims and caprice, they decide to find a new way so that they can fully satisfy their desires and at the same time remain in the fold of Islam and maintain their social standing in society. Therefore, what internally draws them toward deviation is the lack of the spirit of submission and servitude to God and acquiescence to their carnal desires.

In reply to the question on why some people in Islamic society intend to create *fitnah* in religion, Hadrat 'Alī (*'a*) said that the root of all seditions in religion lies in carnal desires which these people cannot abandon. In order to satisfy these desires, they engage in *fitnah* by treading a new way of confronting religious laws and values.

By the way, what is this new way they adopt to advance their objectives? Imām 'Alī (*'a*) said that they formulate laws according to their carnal desires and attribute them to Islam. They engage in distorting the truths of religion by baseless interpretations and false justifications, and interpret the Qur'an and its verses as they wish. As a result, they tell something which is inconsistent with the truth of religion and the Holy Qur'an and encourage the people to disobey the Qur'an. It is evident that these individuals behave in a way that the people do not become aware of their satanic agenda and stop following them.

For Hadrat 'Alī (*'a*) the root of all seditions and innovations in religion is egoism and the lack of the spirit of submission and servitude to God. He (*'a*) also dissuaded the people, especially their leaders, from following their whims and caprice and warned them that the following verse could be applied to them:

﴿ أَرَأَيْتَ مَنِ اتَّخَذَ إِلَٰهَهُ هَوَاهُ ﴾

"Have you seen him who has taken his desire to be his god?"[1]

Those who are today the most influential forces and agents of Satan in distorting religious teachings were not like this to begin with. There are many cases of individuals who were among the upright Muslims and true propagators of the Qur'an and religious teachings, but they changed direction along the way and joined the ranks of the enemies of Islam. They get expelled from the guardianship [*wilāyah*] of God and accept the *wilāyah* and friendship of Satan. On the contrary, there are also many persons who, after many years of deviation and misguiding themselves and others, repent by returning to the fold of Islam and spend the remaining parts of their lives compensating for their undesirable deeds in the past.

This shifting of positions of individuals throughout life is not unusual or uncommon. Yet, what is worthy of note is that according to the Qur'an, there is no sin more dangerous and graver than *fitnah* in religion. The gravest sin is that after knowing the truth and being acquainted with religious laws and teachings, one decides to obstruct people from knowing and acting upon them.

To conclude, I would like to draw the attention of everybody to the precious saying of Hadrat 'Alī (*'a*) when he said:

حَاسِبُوا أَنْفُسَكُمْ قَبْلَ أَنْ تُحَاسَبُوا.

"Take account of your self before you are called to account."[2]

That is, evaluate your self, your beliefs, your ideas, and your actions in the court of your conscience. Before you return to God and lose the opportunity to repent, return to the fold of the Qur'an and the religion of truth. Save yourself from the trap of Satan and the commanding self or carnal soul [*nafs al- 'ammārah*] and frighten it with the inevitable destiny.

Let me conclude with the warning of the Holy Qur'an in this regard when it states, thus:

1 *Sūrah al-Furqān* 25:43.

2 *Bihār al-Anwar*, vol. 8, p. 145.

﴿ ثُمَّ كَانَ عَاقِبَةَ الَّذِينَ أَسَاؤُوا السُّوأَى أَن كَذَّبُوا بِآيَاتِ اللَّهِ وَكَانُوا بِهَا يَسْتَهْزِئُون ﴾

"Then the fate of those who committed misdeeds was that they denied the signs of Allah and they used to deride them."[1]

I implore God, the Exalted, to guide everybody in the path of truth.

﴿ وَالسَّلَامُ عَلَىٰ مَنِ اتَّبَعَ الْهُدَىٰ ﴾

"And may peace be upon him who follows guidance!"[2]

1 *Sūrah al-Rūm* 30:10.

2 *Sūrah TāHā* 20:47.

Index